Colloquial Doesn't Mean Corrupt

STUDIES IN CORNISH LANGUAGE AND CULTURE

Volume 7

STUDIES IN CORNISH LANGUAGE AND CULTURE

A Language Learning to Walk: Cornish in Modern Cornwall (Vol. 9, Ken MacKinnon 2022)

Arthur Symons and his forgotten TRISTAN AND ISEULT (Vol. 8, Alan M. Kent 2021)

Colloquial Doesn't Mean Corrupt (Vol. 7, Rod Lyon 2019)

Otherworlds: Images of Transformation in Cornish Culture (Vol. 6, Brendan McMahon 2016)

Cornish Solidarity: Using Culture to Strengthen Communities (Vol. 5, Neil Kennedy 2016)

Gathering the Fragments: Storytelling and Cultural Resistance in Cornwall
(Vol. 4, Brendan McMahon 2016)

A Wreck upon the Ocean: Cornish Folklore in the Age of the Industrial Revolution
(Vol. 3, Brendan McMahon 2015)

An introduction to the Laws of the Duchy of Cornwall, the Isles of Scilly, and Devon
(Vol. 2, John Kirkhope 2014)

Towards a Cornish Philosophy: Values, Thought, and Language for the West Britons in the Twenty-First Century (Vol. 1, Alan M. Kent, with a foreword by Mathew Staunton 2013)

OTHER BOOKS ABOUT THE CORNISH LANGUAGE FROM EVERTYPE

The Charter Fragment and Pascon agan Arluth (Williams, Everson, Kent 2020)

The Cornish Consonantal System: Implications for the Revival (Nicholas Williams 2016)

Studies in Traditional Cornish (Nicholas Williams, 2016)

Geryow Gwir: The lexicon of revived Cornish (Nicholas Williams 2014)

Desky Kernowek: A complete guide to Cornish (Nicholas Williams 2012)

An Beybel Sans: The Holy Bible in Cornish (tr. Nicholas Williams 2011)

Henry Jenner's Handbook of the Cornish Language (ed. Michael Everson 2010)

Skeul an Tavas: A coursebook in Standard Cornish (Ray Chubb, 2009)

A Concise Dictionary of Cornish Place-Names (Craig Weatherhill, 2009)

Form and Content in Revived Cornish (Everson, Weatherhill, Chubb, Deacon, Williams, 2006)

Towards Authentic Cornish (Nicholas Williams, 2006)

Writings on Revived Cornish (Nicholas Williams, 2006)

Cornish Today (Nicholas Williams, 2006)

STUDIES IN CORNISH LANGUAGE AND CULTURE
Volume 7

Colloquial Doesn't Mean Corrupt

Observations on contemporary Revived Cornish

Rod Lyon

evertype
2019

Published by Evertype, 19A Corso Street, Dundee, DD2 1DR, Scotland. www.evertype.com.

© 2019 Rod Lyon.

First edition 2019. Reprinted October 2021.

Editor: Michael Everson.

All rights reserved. No part of this publication may be reproduced, stored in a retrieval system, or transmitted, in any form or by any means, electronic, mechanical, photocopying, recording, or otherwise, without the prior permission in writing of the Publisher, or as expressly permitted by law, or under terms agreed with the appropriate reprographics rights organization.

A catalogue record for this book is available from the British Library.

ISBN-10 1-78201-246-X
ISBN-13 978-1-78201-246-7

ISSN 2753-1597

Typeset in Baskerville by Michael Everson.

Cover design by Michael Everson, based on a painting of Dolly Pentreath, c. 1777, by John Opie (1761–1807).

TABLE OF CONTENTS

Foreword ix
1 Introduction. 1
2 Context 3
2.1 Survivals of the traditional language. 3
2.2 Jenner and the start of the Cornish revival. 3
2.3 Overlap between middle and Late Cornish 5
2.4 Nance and his approach to Cornish 6
2.5 A. S. D. Smith: Nance's collaborator and critic 6
2.6 The surviving Middle Cornish texts 8
2.7 Smith: Proponent of the medieval language. 9
2.8 Nance's unfortunate legacy. 10
3 Language change 11
3.1 The sound system of traditional Cornish 11
3.2 Unaccented syllables. 12
3.3 The development of Middle Cornish ⟨u⟩ 13
    3.3.1 /y/ unrounded to /i/. 14
    3.3.2 ⟨u⟩, ⟨ue⟩, ⟨eu⟩ /ø/ unrounded to /e/. 15
3.4 The pronunciation of Cornish long *a* 15
3.5 Variation between [z] ⟨s⟩ and [dʒ] ⟨j⟩, ⟨g⟩, ⟨dg⟩. 17
3.6 The alternation *s/j* ignored by Nance 18
3.7 *Nyng* for *nyns* 'not' in Middle Cornish Texts 18
3.8 ⟨Gh⟩ as used in revived Cornish orthography 22
3.9 The Cornish for 'small' as seen in the texts 24
    3.9.1 Forms with *-gh-* 24
    3.9.2 *Byhan, byhen* 24
    3.9.3 *Byan, byen*. 24
    3.9.4 *Bean, vean* 25
    3.9.5 *Bian, bian* 25
3.10 The Cornish for 'small' as seen in place-names 25
3.11 'Horseman, knight' and 'to ride' in Cornish. 27
    3.11.1 'Knight, horseman'. 27
    3.11.2 'Knights, horsemen' 28
    3.11.3 'To ride' (verbal noun) 28
3.12 The Cornish for 'children' in the texts 29
    3.12.1 *Fleghas, fleghes*, etc. with medial *-gh-*. 29
    3.12.2 *Flehas, flehes, flehys* with medial *-h-*. 29
3.13 The Cornish for 'kind, kindred; utmost'. 32
    3.13.1 *Eghen* 32
    3.13.2 *Ehen*. 33
3.14 The Cornish for 'evening'. 33
    3.14.1 *Gorthugher with medial *-gh-*. 34

3.14.2 *Gorthuwher* without medial *-gh-* 34
3.15 The spelling of the word for 'silver' 34
    3.15.1 *Arghans* 34
    3.15.2 *Arhans* 35
    3.15.3 *Arans* 35
3.16 The verb 'to fetch, to bring' 35
    3.16.1 *Kerghes* 35
    3.16.2 *Kerhes* 36
    3.16.2 *Keres* 36
3.17 Loss of final ⟨gh⟩ 36
    3.17.1 *Whe* 'six' 36
    3.17.2 *Saw* 'load' 36
    3.17.3 *Bê* 'burden, load' 37
3.18 The loss of ⟨th⟩ after ⟨r⟩ 38
    3.18.1 *Kerras* for *kerthes* 'to walk' 38
    3.18.2 *In ker* for *in kerdh* 'away' 38
3.19 The phonetics of *r* < *rdh* and *r* < *rth* 39
3.20 Medial *-rth-* reduced to *-r-*, *-rr-* 39
    3.20.1 *Gortheby* 'to answer' > *gorreby* 39
    3.20.2 *Gorrryb* for *gorthyp* 'answer' 40
    3.20.3 *Marrojyon* for *marthojyon* 'wonders' 40
3.21 Final *-gh* written as ⟨th⟩ 40
    3.21.1 *Warlerth* 'after, according to' for *warlergh* 41
3.22 Loss of final ⟨th⟩ [θ] after a vowel 42
3.23 Initial mutations 43
3.24 Absence of initial mutation in place-names 44
3.25 Rhotacization or the shift of [z] > [r] 45
3.26 Pre-occlusion 46
3.27 Pre-occlusion in the 16th and 17th centuries 47
    3.27.1 *Beunans Meriasek* (1504) 47
    3.27.2 Andrew Borde (1547) 47
    3.27.3 *Sacrament an Alter* (c. 1560) 47
    3.27.4 Richard Carew (1602) 47
    3.27.5 *Creation of the World* (1611) 47
    3.27.6 Richard Brome (1632) 49
    3.27.7 Richard Symonds (1644) 49
    3.27.8 Wella Rowe (c. 1680) 49

4 Duals and plurals **51**
4.1 Unattested duals in revived Cornish 51
4.2 The Cornish for 'hands' in the texts 52
    4.2.1 *Dewdhorn* 'hands' (dual) 52
    4.2.2 *Dywla, dewla, dowla* 'hands' (plural) 52
4.3 The Cornish for 'feet' in the texts 54
    4.3.1 *Dewdros* 'feet' (dual) 54
    4.3.2 *Treys* 'feet' (plural) 54

TABLE OF CONTENTS

4.3.3 *Treys ha dewla* 'feet' (plural) and 'hands' (dual) 55
4.4 The Cornish for 'eyes' in the texts 56
    4.4.1 *Dewlagas* 'eyes' (dual) 56
    4.4.2 *Lagasow, lagajow* 'eyes' (plural) 57
4.5 The Cornish for 'legs' in the texts 57
    4.5.1 **Dywarr* 'legs' (dual) 57
    4.5.2 *Garrow* 'legs' (plural) 57
4.6 The Cornish for 'ears' in the texts 58
    4.6.1 **Dywscovarn* 'ears' (dual) 58
    4.6.2 *Scovornow* 'ears' (plural) 58
4.7 The Cornish for 'arms' in the texts 58
    4.7,1 *Dywvregh* 'arms' (dual) 58
    4.7.2 *Brehow* 'arms' (plural) 58
4.8 The Cornish for 'shoulders' in the texts 58
    4.8.1 *Dywscoth* 'shoulders' (dual) 58
    4.8.2 *Scodhow* 'shoulders' (plural) 59
4.9 The Cornish for 'fists, hands' in the texts 59
    4.9.1 *Dewdhorn* 'fists, hands' (dual) 59
    4.9.2 *Dornow* 'fists' (plural) 59
4.10 The Cornish for 'knees' in the texts 59
    4.10.1 *Dewlyn, dowlyn* 'knees' (dual) 59
    4.10.2 *Glinyow* 'knees' (plural) 60
4.11 The Cornish for 'nose, nostrils' in the texts 60
    4.11.1 *Dewfrik* 'nostrils, nose' (dual) 60
    4.11.2 *Frigow* 'nostrils, nose' (plural) 60
4.12 The Cornish for 'thighs' in the texts 60
    4.12.1 **Dywvorthos* 'thighs' (dual) 60
    4.12.2 *Mordhosow* 'thighs' (plural) 60

5 Verbs **61**
5.1 Autonomous forms of the verb 61
    5.1.1 *Pascon agan Arluth* 61
    5.1.2 *Origo Mundi* 62
    5.1.3 *Passio Christi* 62
    5.1.4 *Resurrexio Domini* 62
    5.1.5 *Bewnans Ke* 63
    5.1.6 *Beunans Meriasek* 63
5.2 A construction for indirect statement 64
    5.2.1 Indirect speech with *del* 65
    5.2.2 Indirect speech with *fatel* 65
5.3 Personal forms of the verbal noun *bos* 'to be' 66
    5.3.1 1st person: *bosa, bosaf, bosama* 66
    5.3.2 2nd person: *bota, bosta* 67
    5.3.3 3rd person masculine: *bosa* 67
    5.3.4 3rd person feminine: *bossy* 68
    5.3.5 1st person plural: *bosen* 68

COLLOQUIAL DOESN'T MEAN CORRUPT

    5.3.6 2nd person plural: *bosowgh* 68
    5.3.7 3rd person plural *bosans* 68
  5.4 The pluperfect/conditional 69
  5.5 The imperfect of *godhvos* 'to know' 70
6 Prepositions **71**
  6.1 A personal pronoun ignored by Nance 71
  6.2 *Anjy* 'they' in later texts 72
  6.3 Simplification of prepositional pronouns 73
  6.4 Prepositional pronouns with *the* 'to' 74
    6.4.1 *The vy* 'to me' 74
    6.4.2 *The gy* 'to thee' 74
    6.4.3 *The ny* 'to us, for us' 74
    6.4.4 *The why* 'to you' (plural) 74
    6.4.5 *Thethans, thothans* 'to them' 76
  6.5 Recommended prepositional pronouns 77
    6.5.1 *Dhe* 'to' 77
    6.5.2 *Gans/gen* 'with' 77
    6.5.3 *In* 'in' 77
    6.5.4 *Dhyworth, dhort* 'from' 77
    6.5.5 *Orth* 'at' 78
    6.5.6 *A* 'from, of' 78
    6.5.7 *Wàr* 'upon' 78
    6.5.8 *Rag* 'for' 78
    6.5.9 *Dhyrag, dyrag* 'before, in front of' 78
    6.5.10 *Ryb* 'beside' 78
    6.5.11 *Dre* 'through' 78
7 Problems in the Lexicon **79**
  7.1 *Arhans* 'silver' and *mona* 'money' 79
    7.1.1 *Arhans* 'silver' 79
    7.1.2 *Mona* 'money' 80
  7.2 Spurious coinage 81
  7.3 Questions and answers 82
  7.4 The absurdity of inflectional archaism with modern neologisms ... 84
  7.5 The question of new words 85
8 Counting in Cornish **87**
9 Wella Rowe **93**
  9.1 The Cornish of Wella Rowe 93
  9.2 Rowe's Cornish translation of Genesis 3:1-14 94
  9.3 Rowe's Cornish translation of Matthew 2:1-12 97
10 Summary **101**
Abbreviations **103**
Sources **105**
Symbols **106**
Glossary **108**
Index **111**

FOREWORD

Since the resurrection of Cornish from its deathbed at the start of the 20th century, there have been many enthusiastic attempts to produce a universally accepted and standardized set of grammar books and dictionaries, with each progenitor, by and large, basing his ideals on a specific epoch in the natural development of Cornish. This individual choice of a particular epoch in the language's timeline has, by and large, one serious flaw, and that is, in following this principle, the natural developments which occurred later in the language have been totally disregarded. It is apparent also from studies of each of the individual attempts that an idealistic and pure language has been sought. This, in the author's opinion, has not been achieved but has instead produced an artificial language, as any natural development has been sacrificed to try and produce an uncorrupted pure language.

The original progenitor in the language revival was of course living much closer to the time of the demise of the language, and in fact was in a position to converse with people who actually remembered the language being traditionally spoken. However, his successor, who dedicated the greater part of his life to the slowly growing language movement, was divorced from these people, and so throughout his life chose to produce and advocate this very much idealistic and "pure" Cornish based on the texts of the late 14th century, thus eliminating virtually everything that had evolved in the ensuing years. Unfortunately, subsequent attempts at "rationalizing" or attempting to improve these earlier ideals have still not been achieved, as the disregard for the later, natural developments within the language continues to be very strongly exercised. How can a language be treated as authentic if the clock is turned back so far that any form of natural change is being treated as "incorrect" or "corrupt" and hence systematically dismissed?

Every language through time and usage evolves, and Cornish is no different. How can a language be considered authentic if pronunciations, syntax etc., which were either obsolete or obsolescent in the 14th—and in many instances—the 13th centuries, are resurrected and taught as being correct in a 21st-century language, and in which everything which had transpired in the intervening years is totally disregarded, and if used, strongly condemned? This irrational approach is further compounded in any "conversation" where a modern topic is actually attempted using a 14th-century syntax liberally infused with 21st-century neologisms. It is no different from a conversation in English where Chaucerian syntax and pronunciations are used but with a 21st-century vocabulary. How ridiculous that would sound, but in Cornish it is to all intents and purposes what is being advocated.

In addition, the older texts on which this modern Cornish has been based, are in themselves not conducive to a modern, fluent and lively language, as they are virtually all theological works and in the majority of instances, written in verse. This is very apparent amongst many of those who have learnt their Cornish solely via lessons etc., based on these old texts, archaic or obsolete forms and pronunciations, then try to conduct a modern, interesting or lively conversation. Their speech is dull, slow and lacking any life. Even one of the marginally "later" texts, which clearly shows how the language was evolving—even over the relatively short historical timescale of fifty years—is a theological work. It is not until much later that anything approaching a conversation piece or something of a casual secular nature appears.

There is also the perception in being told that a particular manner of speech adopted outside of that recommended by a language "authority" and its adherents is wrong, smacks of a degree of official language control and regulation.

So, what are all these obsolete or obsolescent syntax forms and spellings—and pronunciations—referred to above, and where are they found? That is what the author has set himself to find out, and these findings are all detailed with hundreds of substantiating examples throughout this book.

Although this research has been conducted over a considerable period of time, the author would like to thank the editor for supplying many further examples and above all for his guidance and patience in further elucidating many grammatical features which the author has not fully analysed or detailed.

Rod Lyon,
Nancegollan, 2019.

1
INTRODUCTION

Every living language changes—rarely by design, but more usually through usage and natural, unplanned development. Cornish should be no different, but those natural changes which occurred over the centuries in Cornish have been largely ignored or rejected by revivalists, and are being replaced by a more doctrinaire form of the language. This purism started in the early twentieth century at the same time as the first serious attempts to revive the language. The leading revivalists believed that Cornish had become so badly debased, that the revived language should reject all corrupt developments. This was an unfortunate decision, given that the ultimate aim was to see the language thrive and have it universally accepted. Regrettably the purists' decision made in the early nineteen hundreds persists in full vigour among many of today's Cornish users.

Professional linguists have over the years criticized today's Cornish as being artificial, largely because of the cavalier disregard for natural development within it and because of the consequent attempts to return to the earliest possible period of the language, when what was believed to be genuine Cornish was spoken. Very many of contemporary Cornish users have been irritated by the criticisms of experts, for they reject the criticisms and consider them wholly unjustified.

One of the most cogent arguments to support the claim that the contemporary language is a construct, involves the use of newly-coined words or neologisms. Neologisms are either words invented *de novo*, borrowed directly from other languages, or as loan-translations or calques on them. However a neologism is formed, it becomes an essential part of a developing language. All languages introduce new words, since such are necessary to enable speakers to talk about a changing world. In the case of a minority language, those coining the new words have to be careful that such items to do not swamp the essential nature of the language. Thus a delicate balance must be struck between re-introducing lexemes that have may have become obsolete on the one hand, and on the other taking care not to overload the language with borrowings from a majority language. It is easy in the case of a minority language to compromise its essential nature by excessive borrowing. English, for example, and other major languages can usually absorb such borrowings without serious difficulty. English after all has over the centuries borrowed so many lexical items from other languages, notably French and Latin, that modern English is very dissimilar from the English of the Anglo-Saxon period. The question of terminology will be dealt with more fully below.

A further and fully justified criticism levelled by linguists at revived Cornish is that it mixes different historical periods of the language. The revivalists retreat as far as they can into to the earliest forms of the language, in an attempt to establish an ideal and uncorrupted form of Cornish, while at the same time using newly coined words to refer to modern objects; and even to use expressions in conversation that would have been quite alien to the medieval language.

So, what, if anything, should be done? Can the status quo with its mixture of eras be justified? Is it feasible to recapture the "purest" form of the language? Or should revivalists rather accept the natural development of the language and agree that such development should be the basis for contemporary Cornish? Is a compromise between the two views possible? The author supports such a middle way. This book will attempt to justify such an approach by means of examples taken from the surviving Cornish texts.

2
CONTEXT

2.1 SURVIVALS OF THE TRADITIONAL LANGUAGE

As has already been noted, the Cornish of today is a revived language. There were a indeed a few tenuous links between the last of those with a traditional knowledge of the language and the start of revival proper in 1904, with the publication of Jenner's *Handbook of the Cornish Language*. Such links, however, are regrettably meagre.

The last reports of Cornish having being spoken naturally, date from the 1860s, for there were reports that (i) Newlyn fishermen would speak Cornish at sea for up to ten minutes at a time and (ii) a personal recollection of Cornish being spoken fairly widely around the same time at Boswednack, near Zennor. The source of the first reference above was from historian Arthur Rablen, who in 1937 interviewed William Botheras, a retired policeman. Further research by the present author revealed that William Botheras, interviewed by Rablen, was referring to his father, also called William, and it was he who went to sea with the fishermen. William Botheras senior was born in 1851 and would probably have been 10 to 12 years of age when he went to sea with the fishermen, that is to say, in the early 1860s. The second report was an interview by Richard Hall of St Just, who spoke to an old man called of John Mann, also of St Just. Mann said that as a boy in Boswednack he knew a "Mrs Berryman who spoke Cornish and that he [Mann] and his companions also spoke it." Mrs Berryman died in 1854 aged 85. We have further and more vague references to Cornish being spoken up until the start of the Revival. Such accounts seem mainly to refer to parents teaching their children the numbers in Cornish, the Lord's Prayer and similar scraps.

2.2 JENNER AND THE START OF THE CORNISH REVIVAL

Although a few amateur philologists and historians dabbled in the language during the nineteenth century, they did nothing of any importance as far as the spoken language was concerned. Henry Jenner was the first to take

§2.2   COLLOQUIAL DOESN'T MEAN CORRUPT

a serious interest in Cornish; and even he in the early days did little more than visit Newlyn and collect a few words. He did not, it seems, investigate any further, since it is known that there were other people alive in West Cornwall at that time and indeed later, who had a knowledge of the language. Such people include John Davey of Boswednak †1891 and Mrs Elizabeth Vingoe of Higher Boswarva, Madron, who lived until 1903. By the end of the nineteenth century, however, Jenner had begun working on the language in earnest and in 1904 (coincidentally only a year after Cornwall was accepted into the Celtic Congress) he published his *Handbook of the Cornish Language*.

On what basis did Jenner research Cornish for this book? Although Celtic linguists at that time attributed eras or periods to the language, for example "Old Cornish", "Middle Cornish" and "Late", or "Modern Cornish", these tended to be rather loosely applied. This approach is unlike the modern practice of regarding them as discrete epochs, in which the language differed widely. This book attempts throughout to show that such an approach is completely mistaken.

Jenner's work and ideas are worth examining in detail. Henry Jenner was born at St Columb in 1848 and as a young man was in a position to hear the remnants of the spoken language which were still in use. This was particularly the case in 1875, when at the age of 27 he visited Newlyn to record Cornish words, etc. Although by that time it is very unlikely that there was much Cornish conversation to be heard, Jenner's informants would still have been producing the natural sounds, intonation and rhythm of the traditional language. As a result he would not have had to theorize about the exact nature of the sounds of Cornish. In this respect he differed greatly from Morton Nance, who was born in Cardiff in 1873 and did not come to Cornwall until 1903. Today's linguists are even more remote from the era of traditional language and thus must depend greatly—too greatly it would seem—on theory.

Jenner therefore having direct personal contact with those who retained the sounds of the traditional language, was better suited than any other revivalist to get right the sounds of Cornish. This will be seen from his *Handbook of the Cornish Language*, to which reference has already been made. The handbook was the first publication aimed at the general reader, rather than at the professional Celtic scholar. Throughout the *Handbook* it is apparent that Jenner had a far better grasp and understanding of the history of Cornish through the centuries until its eventual demise as a spoken language than did his successor, Morton Nance. Nance, although he knew of the developments in Cornish, preferred to ignore many of them. Jenner not only understood such development but actually incorporated them into his book.

2.3 OVERLAP BETWEEN MIDDLE AND LATE CORNISH
Jenner explains quite clearly in his *Handbook* that "Middle Cornish" and "Modern Cornish" cannot not be treated as distinct entities—as is so often the case with the modern revivalists—but that they overlapped. At the same time Jenner hints strongly that there was hardly any colloquial element in the older texts:

> As the whole of extant literature of Middle Cornish is in verse, it gives us little help as regards the colloquial Cornish even of its own period, and judging from Andrew Borde's sentences, only some forty years later than the *St Meriasek* and seventy years earlier than Jordan's play *(Creacion of the World)*, Middle and Modern Cornish must have overlapped one another a good deal. It is probable that those who wrote verse would continue to use archaic forms long after they had been dropped in prose and in conversation. But the difference between Middle and Modern Cornish is not really very great, and comes to very little more than a difference of spelling, an uncertainty about the final letters of certain words, and a tendency to contractions, elisions, and apocopations in words, which, though recognized in their fuller form in the spelling of Middle Cornish verse, may have been nearly as much contracted, elided, and apocopated in Middle Cornish conversation (*Handbook*: 49).

The above quotation from Jenner summarizes very neatly the message of this book, namely that the Cornish advocated today—even in speech—is still too closely based on the rigid diction found in Middle Cornish verse, rather than the spoken Cornish of the same period.

A further valid point was also made by Jenner in his *Handbook* concerning the writings of men such as Boson, Bodinar, Gwavas, etc.:

> These, written by men who spoke Cornish fluently and had no theories and often no knowledge of philology, probably represent what people really spoke in the seventeenth and eighteenth centuries. That faintness and even silence of final letters, which seems to have been a characteristic of Cornish as it is of French, was the cause that, in writing as phonetically as they knew how, these practical speakers of Cornish often omitted the ends of words,

and made it seem as though their verbs had largely lost their inflections (*Handbook*: 52).

2.4 NANCE AND HIS APPROACH TO CORNISH

We can thus see how different was the approach adopted by Jenner to the revival of Cornish from that of his successor, Robert Morton Nance (1873–1959). Nance's attitude was almost diametrically opposed to that of Jenner. Let us, therefore, turn our attention to Nance himself, and glance both at his work and the thinking behind it. As already stated, Nance was born in Wales, of Cornish parents. Nance did not move to Cornwall until 1903, when he settled at Nancledra. It appears that he started to learn Cornish from a copy of William Borlase's *Antiquities*. When, however, he came across Jenner's *Handbook* a little later, he devoured the contents.

Nance met Jenner while they were both doing research in Falmouth and immediately they became friends and began to collaborate on the revival of Cornish. Finally, however, it was Nance himself who through his work on the language elaborated the form of revived Cornish that is most widely promoted today. Nance did an immense amount of work on Cornish. Except perhaps for Jenner, who was very elderly by the time the revival was beginning to take root, Nance was the only person with a knowledge of the language that was thorough enough—and of course with time enough to devote to it—to enable him to synthesize it all and produce a series of dictionaries and grammars. These enabled people to learn to read and write Cornish and in some cases to speak it.

Nance's position as the leading expert on the language created a problem. As far as Cornish was concerned Nance was the prosecution, defence, judge, and jury. In other words, Nance was in a position to do with Cornish exactly what he wanted. This, as history has shown, was in some ways unfortunate. It would seem that Nance in the variety of Cornish he favoured, gave precedence to things which he himself believed *ought to have been* preserved—even though they were unattested—and thus produced a language which was overloaded with spellings and grammatical forms that were obsolete or at least obsolescent even in the earliest Cornish texts. Anything which smacked of change was classed as corrupt and was thus forbidden. Such excluded forms were referred to as "Late Cornish", and indeed they still are.

2.5 A. S. D. SMITH: NANCE'S COLLABORATOR AND CRITIC

The most superficial examination of the medieval texts will reveal Nance's cavalier approach to the revival of the language. A. S. D. Smith (Caradar) collaborated with Nance on Cornish from the nineteen-thirties to the early fifties. Smith was continually criticizing Nance for ignoring or rewriting certain forms which failed to conform to his ideal of perfect Cornish. Unfortunately, Nance had no linguistic training, something which was a huge disadvantage for him when he made the acquaintance of Smith. Smith became interested in Cornish in the nineteen-thirties. He read Latin and Greek in Cambridge, was a fluent Welsh speaker and had alread compiled widely-recommended grammar books for Welsh, when he began to turn his attention to Cornish. With the help of Nance's primer, *Cornish for All*, Smith became fairly fluent in the language. He was a schoolmaster, teaching modern languages. In 1933 he came to Cornwall and was soon working with Nance on the language.

In the course of their work together, Smith had many criticisms and he made many useful suggestions, but Nance always disregarded them and followed his own inclination. The author remembers reading a letter from Smith to Francis Cargeeg after the discovery in 1949 of the Tregear *Homilies*. The Homilies were written c. 1555, slightly after Nance's chosen Middle Cornish period but contained much material to fill in some gaps in Nance's revived Cornish. Nance, however, edited the Cornish of the Tregear manuscript—not only changing all the spelling to his own Unified system, but rewriting the grammatical forms to suit his own idealized Cornish. He thus disregarded the natural development of the language. This caused an outburst from Smith, who was so incensed by Nance that in his letter to Cargeeg, he rather intemperately accused Nance of destroying the traditional language of Tregear's day to suit his own preconceived ideas.

A similar criticism concerning Nance's treatment of William Jordan's *Creation of the World* (CW) was made by Smith in a letter to Nance dated 10th February 1941. In his letter Smith says:

> With regard to the presentation of the Cornish unified text, I find that you have made many changes from the original MS., most of them quite unnecessarily, as I have shown in my notes. I think the original version should be reproduced exactly as it stands, only in Unified spelling: The only changes called for being in a few places, where the text is actually wrong as Cornish...

Later he again writes:

> Another question is whether to preserve certain characteristics peculiar to a late text like CW or bring its Cornish completely into

line, with that of the Ordinalia. You tend towards the latter, but I can't help thinking you go too far.

He gives a few examples, e.g. *deth, be, cows* and *na pell* changed to *duth, bu, kews* and *nep pell*. Of these he says:

> [This] seems to be putting the clock back too far. Likewise, *mara cos'ta, woffya, woffes, 'kyn na'm boma, y vosa* etc. These are all good colloquial forms warranted from the oldest texts, and are a feature of CW. I have shown in my notes that there is nothing wrong with them.

Smith's notes on Nance's revision of *Creation of the World* amounted to 38 pages, just smaller than A4, of close typing. This indicates how exasperated Smith had become with Nance's intrenched attitude to *his* Cornish. We must ask whether Smith's criticisms of Nance's *modus operandi* were really justified. The author's view is that they certainly were, as the briefest examination of the texts will show.

2.6 THE SURVIVING MIDDLE CORNISH TEXTS
Listed here are the texts in chronological order together with their approximate dates. As can be seen they range from the late fourteenth to the early sixteenth century:

1. *Pascon Agan Arluth* (PA) *c.* 1375
2. *The Ordinalia*, consisting of three plays—*Origo Mundi* (OM), *Passio Christi* (PC), and *Resurrexio Domini* (RD), all around 1400
3. *Beunans Meriasek* (BM) 1504.

Together with these one should include:

4. *Bewnans Ke* (BK) *c.* 1500
5. Tregear's Homilies (TH) 1555–1558 together with *Sacrament an Alter* (SA), *c.* 1560,
6. *Creation of the World* (CW) sometimes known as *Gwreans an Bys* 1611.

The last text the above list, *Creation of the World*, was in Nance's mind, definitely outside his optimum period. It dated, however, from a time 300 years before he introduced his Unified Cornish, and about 400 years before today's modern standardized Cornish. Strictly speaking, however, it was only slightly later than the generally accepted Middle Cornish period.

Tregear's *Homilies* were even less outside of Nance's optimum period—by barely 50 years—but they were written in a more colloquial style, representing as they do the spoken language of the time. They display more features of the developing language and as such were unacceptable to Nance's vision of a perfect medieval language—hence Smith's outburst to which reference is made above.

2.7 SMITH: PROPONENT OF THE MEDIEVAL LANGUAGE

Smith himself, even though he envisaged that Cornish would be spoken again, was also in a way rooted in the Middle Ages, as can be seen from the closing paragraph in his little book *The Story of the Cornish Language* where he says,

> The decline of Cornish in the 18th century need not be regretted. Had the language survived into modern times, it would inevitably have lost much of its own idiom owing to the overwhelming influence of English, and its vocabulary would have become more English than Cornish. As it is, we have a compact medieval language, whose idiom is Celtic and little likely to undergo further changes; and we can take heart at the thought that what we now write in Cornish will be as fully intelligible 1,000 years hence as it is in the present year of grace 1947.

The somewhat remarkable fact however is that the official bodies—and some not so official bodies—promoting today's Standard Written Form still essentially advocate Nance's ideals and, like him, dismiss anything in syntax or inflection that occurs in anything later than *Bewnans Ke* or *Beunans Meriasek*. Whereas Nance, at least in his first 1938 Cornish-English Dictionary, did include many later Cornish alternatives and examples, in today's Standard Written Form, these are all ignored. In 1941 A. S. D. Smith criticized Nance for "going back too far" in his approach to revived Cornish, but it seems that the modern approach to elaborating a standardized Cornish is equally culpable, if not more so. If any feature is mentioned, which can be found among the developments that are actually attested in Middle Cornish texts and are discussed below, it will be condemned in very much the same way as Nance's condemnation of them. Such developments are repudiated as late corruptions from West Cornwall. It is apparent, however, to anyone who takes the trouble to examine the Middle Cornish texts, that the same developments were well established in the early texts. They are in no sense Late Cornish corruptions!

§2.8 COLLOQUIAL DOESN'T MEAN CORRUPT

As Jenner points out, the Middle Cornish texts were written in verse and thus were largely lacking in the colloquial and racy nature of everyday speech. As a result contemporary Cornish, and in particular spoken Cornish, is almost always so stilted, for it is almost entirely based on the constructions and phraseology of theological discourse, rather than on the everyday spoken Cornish of the time. The language of the medieval plays is thus very unlike that of the later writing. Although the later texts are largely ignored by today's revivalist, to incorporate their diction into the revived language would certainly give it a more colloquial flavour. And let us not forget that the later texts are themselves now 300 years old!

2.8 NANCE'S UNFORTUNATE LEGACY

Returning now to Nance and his early work on the language revival, we can ask what were the natural developments which he ignored and what unjustified purisms did he import into the language? As we shall see many of them have been perpetuated and are now an obstacle both to the authenticity of the revived language and an unnecessary complication in the path of learners.

The most common of Nance's infelicities can be listed as follows:

- Retention of unstressed vowels
- Maintenance of quiescent letters in spellings like *byghan* 'small', *marghak* 'knight', etc.
- Unwarranted changes in spelling
- Disregard of analogical forms in personal and prepositional pronouns
- Disregard of simplification in prepositional pronouns
- Archaism in indirect statement
- Repudiation of pre-occlusion
- The recommendation of unattested dual forms.
- Archaizing inflection

These will all be examined in turn in the following pages.

3
LANGUAGE CHANGE

3.1 THE SOUND SYSTEM OF TRADITIONAL CORNISH

An important part of modern standardized Cornish which is at variance with the natural development of the language is to be seen in the pronunciation. Much thought and research in some quarters has gone into what is considered the correct sound system of Middle Cornish. Why should this be? Why was it necessary? To the present author this search for the so-called true pronunciation is a retrograde step, since one is attempting to turn the clock back instead of moving forward with it. The most superficial examination of the later writers in Cornish will show immediately that significant changes in pronunciation had occurred. Why should we not accept them as spontaneous developments in the language? Why is it necessary to search for some hypothetically perfect diction, which may or may not have existed several centuries ago?

The pronunciation which has been derived from this research may indeed give a close approximation to the way words were pronounced in one area of Cornwall at one particular period. It is probable, however, that there would have been differences even over relatively small distances. Since the language was undergoing continuous change, there would not have been any actual standard to follow. Even in the Middle Cornish texts, different scribes within the same document exhibit different styles, forms and spellings.

The hypothetical phonology of recent research is now a serious problem, for it appears that such phonology is taking the revived language further and further from the traditional language. As a result contemporary revivalists are less and less likely even to try to imitate the phonology of the traditional language. Indeed many people nowadays, particularly those who have recently started to learn the language, are exaggerating the distance between pronunciations accepted in the early days of the revival and those which are promoted today as being correct. In which case, a question immediately arises: How can a revived language claim to be authentic, if natural shifts and developments in it are considered to have been incorrect and corrupt? How can such a laguage be considered authentic, if the only evidence for it was written in the earliest texts, in verse, and with very little in it to suggest the spoken vernacular? My point is exemplified by the difference between *Beunans Meriasek* written in 1504 and Tregear's *Homilies* written only about 50 years later. The Homilies certainly do not reflect entirely the contemporary vernacular, but they are noticeably more informal and colloquial than *Beunans Meriasek*.

Why do we need continually to invoke the vernacular? Quite simply no language is of much use if it is not spoken—and spoken with at least a modicum of passion and vigour. Language is what the word itself describes—a tongue—a term still used as such in the context of a spoken language in particular. Indeed in many languages the word for "tongue" refers both to the organ of the body and to the language itself. Let us now look at some examples of these modern pronunciations and examine how theory has divorced them in significant ways from the sounds actually produced by the speakers of traditional Cornish.

3.2 UNACCENTED SYLLABLES

Among the commonest unaccented syllables are the monosyllabic particles *a*, *y* and *ow*. The particle *a* occurs in verbal constructions such as *me a wra mos* 'I shall go' and *ev a welas an den* 'he saw the man'. Although it is usually written, the *a* of the particle would hardly have been noticed in speech. The two phrases above should not be spoken with clear breaks between the *me* the *a* and *wra*—*me-a-wra*, as is so often heard, but *meawra*, spoken as though it were one unit but with the stress on the *me*. Similarly the second phrase—*evawelas*—should be spoken as one word but with the stress on the *ev*. This is not bad grammar or elocution, it is customary in conversation, since reduction of unstressed syllables is usual in many languages. Let us look at the question, *a wrusta mos?* 'did you go?' This again is not spoken as *a-wrus-ta-mos* but almost as *wrusta mos?* with the interrogative particle *a* hardly audible.

The particle *y* is even more weakly pronounced than the particle *a*. Many learners conscientiously pronounce it as though it were the dominant portion of the phrase. How often has one heard *yma* pronounced as **ee**ma? For example the simple sentence *yma meur a dus i'n hel* 'there are many men in the hall' should not be pronounced **ee**ma-meur-a-dus-i'n-hel, but simply, *ma meur adus i'n hel*. This also applies to other tenses and combinations involving the particle *y*. *Yth esa meur a dus...* 'There were many men...' is not pronounced *eeth-esa-meur-a-dus...*' with each individual syllable pronounced separately, but run more together and with the initial ⟨y⟩

virtually omitted: *thesa meuradus*..... Moreover the weakened pronunciation of the particle *y* applies in all cases. For example, *ev a leverys y teuth* 'he said that he came' should not be pronounced as *ev-a-leverys-ee-teuth*, but as *evaleverys yteuth*, with the *y* being pronounced as a barely perceptible *uh* joined to *teuth*.

It should be remembered, of course, that *y* is weakly pronounced *only* if it is the verbal particle; the possessive adjective *y* 'his' is not to be so weakly pronounced.

The the common plural possessive adjectives *agan*, *agas* and *aga* are invariably today pronounced with the emphasis on the initial *a*, i.e., ˈ*agan*, ˈ*agas* and ˈ*aga*. A cursory look though later written Cornish will reveal that very many instances, these were written *gan*, *gas* and *ga* respectively. This indicates clearly that the emphasis was on the second syllable rather than on the first. And indeed this was particularly noticeable when a post-posited emphatic pronoun was included in the phrase, e.g. *agas eskyjyow why* 'your shoes' being pronounced as *gas skyjyow why*.

The author was in conversation with a Welsh-speaking school teacher some years ago and was told that in his school in Wales the trend, particularly with pupils at school, was very much as in the example above. He said that one morning a pupil turned up at school without his school bag, and when asked *Ple ma dha sagh?* 'Where is your bag?' (the Cornish equivalent is given here), the boy replied, *Ma sagh vy war an bùss* omitting the possessive adjective *ow* 'my' before the *sagh* 'bag' and simply using the emphatic post-posited *vy*. This is precisely what is found in traditional Late Cornish. In fact, as noted by Jenner, the use of the post-posited emphatic pronoun instead of the possessive adjective was probably not restricted to the later era, but the general trend throughout the centuries of spoken Cornish; it simply appeared in the later period, as people were writing in the way in which they spoke (probably the only way they knew) rather than writing literary Cornish.

3.3 THE DEVELOPMENT OF MIDDLE CORNISH ⟨U⟩

Examination of the Middle Cornish indicates that ⟨u⟩ was usually the spelling for the vowel [yː] in *tus* 'men', *gul* 'to do', etc. By the time of the later writers, tha same vowel was most frequently written ⟨i⟩ or ⟨ee⟩. At first glance it might seem that Middle Cornish [y(ː)] had become [i(ː)] by the Late Cornish period. It is likely, however, that the unrounded pronunciation was already well established in Middle Cornish. There are several reasons to believe this to be the case. In the first place the Welsh cognate of *tus* 'men' is *tud* and which is pronounced with an unrounded vowel [i(ː)] or [i(ː)]. Similarly in the Cornish place-name *Luxulyan* < *Lok*

§3.3.1   COLLOQUIAL DOESN'T MEAN CORRUPT

Sulyan, the stressed vowel of the second element is written ⟨u⟩ but pronounced as though it were ⟨i⟩. Moreover Tregear on occasion writes *wrug* 'did' as ⟨rig⟩. The verbal noun *gul* is written ⟨gîl⟩ by Lhuyd and ⟨gweel⟩ by Nicholas Boson. When all this evidence is taken together, it is virtually certain that *tus* and *gul* should be pronounced as /tiːz/ and /giːl/ or /gwiːl/ in the revived language. Unfortunately many newly-recruited Cornish learners are now pronouncing the vowel in *tus*, *gul*, etc. with the vowel of English *cute*!

The same graph ⟨u⟩ is sometimes used in Middle Cornish to represent the rounded mid-high front vowel /ø/. This is approximately the sound in French *cœur* 'heart' or *sœur* 'sister'. In Cornish this sound often written ⟨eu⟩ and ⟨ue⟩, for example *leun* 'full' in PA and *luen* in the Ordinalia. Nance, incidentally, did not realize that ⟨u⟩, ⟨eu⟩, ⟨ue⟩ in the Middle Cornish texts represented two quite separate sounds. As a result, in Unified Cornish [døːs] 'come!' and the second element in [i dyːs] 'his men' are written identically in Unified Cornish as ⟨dus⟩. It should be noted, however, that when [øː] unrounds, it becomes a long closed *e* [eː]. This is approximately the sound in French *blé* 'corn' or *pré* 'meadow'. In Cornish is was often written ⟨e⟩ (or sometimes even as ⟨ee⟩). This unrounding is apparent in many Middle Cornish texts. Tregear always writes *leun* 'full' as ⟨lene⟩. In *Bewnans Ke* 'come' is variously written ⟨duus⟩, ⟨dus⟩, ⟨dys⟩, ⟨des⟩, ⟨dees⟩. In PA a *vu, y fu* 'was' appears as a *ve, y fe*; and *a thue* 'comes' as *a the*. The place-name *Tresmeer* < *Ros Muer* is attested as early as 1284. In place-names /ø/ when unrounded on occasion appears as ⟨eo⟩. The shift of /ø/ ⟨u⟩, ⟨eu⟩, ⟨ue⟩ to /e/ ⟨e⟩, far from being a Late Cornish corruption was attested in Northeast Cornwall at the end of the thirteenth century!

Here are two lists of place-names. In the first list A. are toponyms containing ⟨u⟩ /y/ which unrounds to /i/. In the second B are names which contain ⟨u⟩, ⟨eu⟩, ⟨ue⟩ /ø/ which unrounds to /e/, written ⟨e⟩, ⟨ee⟩, ⟨eo⟩. In the two lists A and B the contemporary name is cited first, followed by the parish (in parentheses); then the earliest attested spelling with unrounding, and finally the etymological form.

3.3.1 /y/ unrounded to /i/
Polpear (Lelant): Polpeer (1356) < *pol pur* 'clean pool'
Tencreek (Menheniot): Trencryke (1495) < *tre an crug* 'farm at the barrow'
Trencreek (Veryan): Trencrig (1340) < *tre an crug* 'farm at the barrow'
Trencreek (Creed): Trenkrek (1370) < *tre an crug* 'farm at the barrow'.

Notice also the modern place-names Tencreek (Lansallos) < *keyn crug* 'ridge barrow' and Tencreek (St Veep) < *tre an crug* 'farm at the barrow'.

3.3.2 ⟨u⟩, ⟨ue⟩, ⟨eu⟩ /ø/ unrounded to /e/

Minnimeer (Tremaine): Menamer (1201) < *meneth meur* 'great hill'
Polgreen (St Veep): Polgrein (c. 1250) < *pol greun* 'grain pool'
Tresmeer (Tresmeer): Tresmere (1284) < *tre Wasmeur* 'Gwasmeur's farm'
Trevear (Sennen): Treveer (1335) < *tre veur* 'great farm'
Nancemeor (St Clements): Nansmeor (1340) < *nans meur* 'great valley'
Carvear (St Blazey): Carveor (1391): < *ker veur* 'great fort'
Tregoose (Feock): Tregose Veer (c. 1400) < *tre goos veur* 'great wood farm'
Duporth (St Austell): Deweporthmeor (1428) < *dew borth meur* 'great two coves'
Trevorva (Probus): Treworvowe Veor (1430) < *tre Worvo veur* 'Gorvo's great farm'
Polgrain (St Wenn): Polgren Vyan (1449) < *pol greun vian* 'small grain pool'
Dunmeer (Bodmin): Dunmere (1459) < *dyn meur* 'large fort'
Trewirgie (Redruth): Trewythgy Veor (c. 1470) < *tre Wythgi veur* 'Guidgi's great farm'
Treweeg (Stithians): Trewyke Meer (c.1474) < *tre wig veur* 'great churchtown farm'
Tolgus (Redruth): Talgoys Mere (c. 1475) < *tol goos meur* 'great hole-wood'.

Again it can legitimately be asked why is a spontaneous development in Cornish ignored in the interest of a phantom purity? Late Cornish developments are in so many cases already established in the earliest Middle Cornish. This book is written in Modern English. Perhaps the purists would prefer to see it written in Chaucerian English.

3.4 THE PRONUNCIATION OF CORNISH LONG A

Some modern revivalist recommend that historical long *a* in Cornish, for example, in *tas* 'father', *pras* 'meadow', *brâs* 'great', *cân* 'song', and *gwâv* 'winter' should be pronounced [ɑː], i.e. with the vowel heard in Standard English father, etc. This is a serious and most regrettable mistake, and has come about as a result of over-reliance on comparison with Breton and Welsh.

Cornish long *a* should have two pronunciations: A. it should be pronounced as a back *a* [ɒː] or open *o* [ɔː] before *n* and *l* in some monosyllables, e.g. in *cân* 'song' and *tâl* 'forehead'. It also has a back pronunciation in the vicinity of *b*, for example in the word *brâs* 'big' and after *w*, e.g. in *gwâv* 'winter'; B. elsewhere in monosyllables historic long *a* is raised to [æː] or even [ɛː], e.g. *tas* 'father', *fas* 'face', and *glas*, blue', *whath* 'still, yet'.

§3.4 COLLOQUIAL DOESN'T MEAN CORRUPT

The evidence for the raised back pronunciation in A. is unmistakable. Nicholas Boson spells *cân* 'song' as ⟨caon⟩; Gwavas writes ⟨broaz⟩ for *brâs* and John Boson writes ⟨brose⟩. That this is a well-established feature of Cornish can be seen from the spelling ⟨brosyen⟩ 'important people', the plural of *bras*, in *Beunans Meriasek* (BM 3215). On the other hand the pronunciation of long *a* as [æː] or [ɛː] began in Middle Cornish, as can be seen from the common spelling ⟨wheth⟩ for 'yet' in the Ordinalia, and the spelling ⟨feth⟩ for 'face' as early as the *Pascon agan Arluth*. Lhuyd's word for 'bitch' is *gest*, which corresponds with W *gast*, which would seem to indicate that the long *a* in the word has been raised to [ɛː]. Furthermore place-names like *Creeglaze* < *Crug Glas and Pol Glaze* < *Poll Glas* indicate that the long a in speech has a raised pronunciation.

Three points need to be stressed in this context:

1. The raising of [aː] > [æː] or [ɛː] has nothing at all to do with any similar development in English, although it is sometimes erroneously linked to the series of changes in the English sound-system known as the Great Vowel Shift. Languages, even those in close contact, do not usually borrow phonetic changes wholesale from each other. This is likely to be true in the case of Middle English and Middle Cornish. The Great Vowel Shift affected all the English long vowels, yet it is never suggested that all the Cornish long vowels were similarly affected by the English shift. Moreover the raising of long *a* is widespread in other languages. It occurs, for example, in some South Welsh dialects and in a wide swathe of territory in Mid Wales (notably in that part of the Welsh-speaking area from which Edward Lhuyd came). Moreover a similar raising of long *a* is normal in the Irish dialects of the North-West of Ireland. There is no need to invoke the English Great Vowel Shift to explain a pronunciation similar to English *glaze* of Cornish *glas* 'green'
2. When Cornish long a was raised it became [æː] or [ɛː]. There is no evidence at all to suggest that the resulting segment was a diphthong [ei], seen for instance in Standard English *gate, hate*.
3. It is sometimes suggested that the Middle Cornish spelling ⟨ay⟩, for example, in *tays* 'father', *glays* 'green', *rays* 'grace', etc. is an indication that the vowel has been raised from [aː] > [æː] or ɛː]. Such a suggestion is unlikely to be true. The use of ⟨y⟩ in the combination ⟨ay⟩ is almost certainly as a marker of length. Although *tays* in *Pascon agan Arluth* and *Beunans Meriasek* almost certainly had a raised vowel, the ⟨y⟩ in the spelling was not intended to show that raising. Rather, it indicated length. This can be seen from the similar spellings in ⟨oy⟩

indicating long [oː] in *boys* 'to be' at PA 49b, 110b, 1222a, BM 315, 522, 747; *doys* 'to come' PA 171b, BM 457, 610, 796, 869 and *moys* 'to come' BM 467, 689, 733, 706, 1079.

3.5 VARIATION BETWEEN [Z] ⟨S⟩ AND [DƷ] ⟨J⟩, ⟨G⟩, ⟨DG⟩

One significant feature of the language which can be seen in the earliest Middle Cornish texts was the use of [dʒ], written ⟨g⟩, ⟨gg⟩, or ⟨dg⟩ in some words, when [z] written ⟨s⟩ was also often used in the same words, for example, *gallosek* 'powerful' RD 2394 but *gallogek* RD 2376; *pysy* 'to pray' PC 37 but *pygy* PC 1013; *bohosogyon* 'poor people' BM 2551 but *bohogogyon* BM 4204. The variation was probably dialectal, but it is likely that the variation was also found in the speech of individuals. This variation occurs only when the *s* or *g* derives from Old Cornish *d*. It appears that first of all the *d* was assibilated to [dz]. This is the sound heard, for example, in English *suds*, *beds*, *odds* and *adze*. The [dz] then in some dialects or forms of Cornish simplified. The first element was lost and thus [dz] became simple [z], written ⟨s⟩. This accounts for the ⟨s⟩ in *gallosek, pysy* and *bohosogyon*. In other dialects, before the cluster [dz] could simplify to [z], the second element was palatalized from [z], the sound in English *lazy*, *hazy*, *easy*, to [ʒ]. This latter is the sound in English *leisure*, *pleasure*, *treasure*, etc. The ensuing consonant cluster was [dʒ], which is precisely the sound heard in English *badger*, *magic*, *sojourn*, etc. Thus from Old Cornish *d* are derived two sounds. One is written ⟨s⟩ and the other appears as ⟨g⟩ or ⟨gg⟩, and on occasion ⟨j⟩. Later it is sometimes written ⟨dg⟩.

Two points should be noted here. In the first place the assibilation of *d* is unique to Cornish, since it does not occur in either Welsh or Breton. Secondly, [z] written ⟨s⟩ did not develop into [dʒ] written ⟨g⟩, etc. The two differing developments were contemporaneous. From a phonetic point of view, it is difficult to see how a simple voiced sibilant [z] could acquire a stopped pronunciation, that is to say, how it could acquire a [d] before it.

There are, however, two stronger reasons for believing that there was no alleged development of [z] to [dʒ]. In the first place forms in ⟨g⟩ occur in the earliest remains of Middle Cornish. As we shall see below, ⟨g⟩ forms are already the norm in *Pascon agan Arluth*, the earliest long text in Middle Cornish. If the putative shift of [z] to [dʒ] had really occurred, it would have been expected to be universal. All examples of [z] ought to have become [dʒ] in Cornish. Where [z], however, had not arisen from an earlier [d], it remained [z] and did not undergo any change. Thus Thomas Boson writes *preezyo* 'praise!' (pl.), *couzas* 'spoke'; John Boson writes *signezou* 'signs'; Wella Rowe writes *desyryes* 'desired', *dezerio* 'desires', *a gowzas* 'spoke', *e cowzaz* 'spoke', *cowsez* 'spoken', *composez* 'accomplished', *eglezow* 'churches' and Lhuyd writes *enèzou* 'islands', *izal* 'low', *kazak* 'mare', *kozal* 'quiet', *kouza* 'to speak' and *lyzûan* 'plant'. If [z] had actually become [dʒ], Thomas Boson's *preezyo* 'praise!' (pl.) would have been *preegyo, and Rowe's *composez* and *composa* would have been *compoges and *compoga respectively. Similarly, the place-name *Jerusalem*, so spelt by Rowe several times, would have been *Jerugalem or *Jerujalem and his word *roza* 'nets' would have been *roga.

3.6 THE ALTERNATION *S/J* IGNORED BY NANCE

These alternation *s/j* seems to be a bone of contention among contemporary language organizations, but it was an essential and natural development in Cornish. Forms in ⟨g⟩, ⟨gg⟩, and ⟨j⟩ were in existence in the earliest texts. They were not late corruptions. Again one is compelled to ask why are the ⟨g⟩ forms either ignored or condemned?

As we have seen in the previous section the variant reflexes of assibilation of [d] in words like *nyns/nyng* 'not', *usy/ujy*, *crysy/cryjy* 'to believe', etc., are not a function of chronology. The two variants emerged at the same time but in different dialects.

Nance never really accepted spellings with ⟨g⟩ in some words and this dislike of such variants has persisted until the present day. Nance's apparent avoidance of forms like *nyng*, *nynj* for *nyns* 'not', *nanj* for *nans* 'now, already, *kerenja* for *kerensa* 'love', *cryjy*, *crejy* for *crysy*, *cresy* 'to believe', *pyjy*, *pejy* for *pysy*, *pesy* 'to pray' and *ujy* for *usy* 'is' can be ascribed to his purism. Because forms with *g* or *j* in *kerenga*, *pygy* and *ugy* appear to predominate in Late Cornish, Nance mistakenly believed that they were late corruptions. In fact, as mentioned, the two forms *kerensa* and *kerenja* are of exactly the same age, representing as they do two different variants of the same original form. Nance's reluctance to countenance in Unified Cornish forms like *nynj o*, *nanj o*, *ujy*, *pyjy*, etc. is all the more perplexing when one remembers how prevalent such forms are in *Pascon agan Arluth*, which was Nance's foundation text. To a large extent forms in ⟨g⟩ rather than ⟨s⟩ seem to predominate in the western dialects of Cornish. *Pascon agan Arluth* is usually associated with Sancreed in the far west of Cornwall. It is not astonishing therefore that the text should exhibit a marked preference for ⟨g⟩ forms. Indeed in *Pascon agan Arluth*, *nyns* 'not' before vowels in *bos* 'to be' and *mos* 'to go' is entirely absent; *nyng* (i.e. *nynj*) is found in the text more than 25 times.

3.7 *NYNG* FOR *NYNS* 'NOT' IN MIDDLE CORNISH TEXTS

Listed below are all the forms of *nyng* with ⟨g⟩ or ⟨j⟩ from the various Middle Cornish texts. Note first that *nyni o* is a medieval spelling for *nynj o*; second that in the following list word division is editorial:

*pan yn provas **nyni** o man* 'when he tried it is was not at all' PA 6d
*henna ganso **nyni** o poys* 'that was not difficult for him' PA 10b
*ym meȝens y forth **nyng** es* 'they said: there is no way' PA 32d
*den vyth **nyng** es yn meȝy* 'there is nobody, she said' PA 34c
*byth **nyng** ens y coweȝe* 'they were never companions' PA 41ab
*mas **nyni** ough ol da na whek* 'but you are not all good or sweet' PA 47b
*yn tre vyth y **nyng** ens gyw ȝe weȝyll dris y vynnas* 'in nothing were they fit to do contrary to his desire' PA 68d
*gallus **nyng** ese kemmen* 'there was no way at all' PA 75b
***nyng** yw mernas belyny* 'it is merely savagery' PA 82d
*In meth Ihesus **nyng** vgy ow mesternges yn bys ma* 'Christ said, my lordship is not in this world' PA 102a
***nyng** ew ragos se laȝe Cryst yv synsys mur dremas* 'it is not your job to kill Christ who is considered a great good man' PA 123bc
*byth reson ȝe laȝe **nyng** es keffys* 'no reason at all has been found to kill him' PA 128d
*ogas o **nyng** esa pell* 'it was near, it was not far' PA 140b
*en grows whath **nyni** o parys* 'the cross was not yet ready' PA 151c
*Whath kentrow ȝeȝe **nyng** o* 'Still they had no nails' PA 154a
*bytegyns byth **nyng** ese* 'nonetheless it was not there' PA 157b
***nyng** ew ow faynys beghan* 'my pains are not slight' PA 166b
*rag kerensa **nyni** o ken* 'for love, it was not otherwise' PA 167d
*scyle **nyn** io nagonon* 'there was no cause at all' PA 187d
*ynno eff dyfout **nyng** es* 'in him there is no fault' PA 192c
*ha **nyni** o hard ȝy notye* 'and he was not brave enough to announce it' PA 214d
*ha ynno **nyni** o parys den marow rag receve newyth parrys **nyni** o vsijs* 'and it was not ready to receive a dead man, newly prepared it had not been used' PA 233ab
*eff **nyni** o hardh ȝy notya* 'he was not brave enough to announce it' PA 234b
***nyng** es forth ȝe omweȝe* 'there is no way to protect ourselves' PA 245d
*whath yn er na **nyng** ens war* 'still at that time they were not aware' PA 252d
*vmma **nyng** ew ef tregis* 'here he does not dwell' PA 255d
*a **nyng** ese alwheow warbarth yn ages guyth why* 'were the keys not together in your keeping?' PC 650-51
*so whath **nyng** ew mas vn du* 'but yet there is only one God' TH 1a
*na neill **nyng** o dyag the wull obereth da* 'neither was he slow to do good works' TH 2a
*Rag **nyng** esan ny ow cara Du* 'For we do not love God' TH 9a
*inweth **nyng** o mab den abyll the weras y honyn in hemma* 'moreover mankind were not able to help themselves in this matter' TH 12-12a

§3.7 COLLOQUIAL DOESN'T MEAN CORRUPT

Rag henna **nyng** *one ny mymbers with anotho eff* 'Therefore we are not any members of his' TH 24

nyng *ew thyn entent na* 'it is not for that purpose' TH 55a

thotheff **nyng** *ew tra vith impossible* 'to him nothing is impossible' TH 56a

nyng *ew nebas an honour ew reys thagen ganow* 'not slight is the honour given to our mouth' SA 59a

nyng *o ef only deane ew sacrificed* 'he was not only man that was sacrificed' SA 61

nyng *us gesis tellar veth* 'no place is left' SA 61

nyng *o Corf Christ kyns ef the vos consecratis* 'it was not the body of Christ before it was consecrated' SA 62

An Discipels **nyng** *o abel thy gyrreow age arluth Christ* 'The disciples were not ready for the words of their lord Christ' SA 62a

shap a gois **nyng** *ew gwelis* 'the form of blood is not seen' SA 63

Dir henna **nyng** *ew gois Christ abhorris* 'Thus the blood of Christ is not abhorred' SA 63

rag **nyng** *o met ef the deserya mas e bask e honyn* 'for it was not meet for him to desire anything but his own Passover' SA 64a

ema ran **nyng** *egy ow tybbry corf Christ thaga sawya ha rag henna* **nyng** *ew thethans corf Dew* 'there are some who do not consume the Body of Christ to save them and therefore they have not the body of God' BSA 65a

nyng *ew dir hastenab apoyntis* 'it was not instituted hurriedly' SA 66

Bara **nyng** *ew figure* 'Bread is not a symbol' SA 66a

Nyng *ew repref tho'm ehan* 'There is no reproof to my kin' BK 96

Nyng *es Du saw onyn lel* 'There is no God but one truly' BK 136

nyng *egas in fas war the forth hyr* 'you are not in a good way in the long run' BK 168-69

Ow galarow **nyng** *yns lowes* 'My sorrows are not limp' BK 181

Nyng *es gwyer Thew saw onyn* 'There is no true God but one' BK 194

hag indella **nyng** *ew vas* 'and thus it is not good' BK 295

Nyng *uge heb galarow* 'He is not without affliction' BK 340

Ow maw **nyng** *ewgy gena'* 'My servant is not with me' BK 453

Dar, **nyng** *ewa dyenys in mosogter ow penys* 'What, he is not gasping while fasting in a stench' BK 507-08

nyng *es drog na galaraw the'n fals a scornyas ow du* 'there is no ill or torment affecting the renegade who scorned my god' BK 524-25

nyng *ew ken the accowntya agys guthyl e thesyr* 'there is nothing to be considered than to do his desire' BK 540-41

nyng *ew henna mars pen cog* 'that man is nothing but a blockhead' BK 544

Nyng *ew thynny gul both e vrys* 'It is not for us to do the will of his heart' BK 737-38

LANGUAGE CHANGE §3.7

Lemmyn **nyng** *ew vas an towl* 'Now the plan is not good' BK 769
nyng *es thenny mar tha car* 'we have not such a good friend' BK 828
Bonas mata the bagan **nyng** *ew rago'* 'It is not for me to be the friend of a pagan' BK 919-20
nyng *ew guyw the vorogath* 'he is not worthy to ride out' BK 929
Nyng *ew ragtha in certan bos mata thew'* 'It is not for him indeed to be a friend to you' BK 943-44
Nyng *ew ragtha in certan* 'It is not for him indeed' BK 952
Don e sor **nyng** *ew mar scaf* 'To bear his anger is not so easy' BK 997
nyng *ew marth kyn fen methak* 'it is no wonder, though I am ashamed' BK 1012
Nyng *es ysmek a'ga far* 'There is no lotion equal to them' BK 1122
Nyng *es ewyth in the vody* 'There is no vigour in your body' BK 1244-45
Nyng *es myghtern in neb gwlas na wothvean, rennothas! dystogh lyha e vrusyl* 'There is no king in any country whose insubordination by my father, I could not immediately reduce' BK 1305-07
Nyng *es mar tha kenwesow in chy arluth i'n bys ma* 'There are not such good feasts in the house of any lord in this world' BK 1310-11
Nyng *es myghtern mar rial in dan nef heb dowt i'n cas* 'There is not such a regal king under heaven without doubt in the matter' BK 1314-15
Peb a'th wormol, **nyng** *es dowt* 'All men praise you, there is no doubt' BK 1966
nyng *es orthes rag perel mars an emprowr, agan arluth* 'there is no danger for you but the emperor, our sovereign' BK 1881-93
rag **nyng** *yw vas* 'for it is not good' BK 2206
By my soul! **nyng** *eth the gol meugh a ros a the thega* 'By my soul! the pledge he gave as tithe has not been lost' BK 2247-48
Nyng *yw y daul gortheby* 'It is not his plan to answer' BK 2293
Nyng *es den mar stowt* 'There is no man so stalwart' BK 2483
In dan an howl **nyng** *es gowr a'gas feth bys venari* 'There is no hero under the sun who will ever defeat you' BK 2540-41
ha gortas da **nyng** *ew hyer* 'and a good wait is not long' BK
rag ef a verew, **nyng** *es dowt, mar pith kevys ugh an dor* 'for he will die, there is no doubt, if he is found above the earth' BK 2792-93
Tribut nahen **nyng** *es* 'There is no other tribute' BK 28670
Nyng *ew ow thowl servya an Jowl* 'It is not my plan to serve the Devil' BK 2937-38
Nyng *ew dever* 'It is not a duty' BK 2957
nyng *ew guew the varogath* 'he is not worthy to ride out' BK 3277
ragtha warthy **nynj** *ew ef* 'he is not worthy of it' CW 263

§3.7　COLLOQUIAL DOESN'T MEAN CORRUPT

Nyng *es goon heb lagas na kei heb scovern* 'There is no down without an eye nor hedge without an ear' WScawen

Nyng *es travith dale talues en beez...* 'There is nothing which should be valued in the world...' NBoson.

One thing is clear from these examples. *Nyng, nynj* 'are in no sense late corruptions. On the contrary, they are an essential feature of the language from the earliest Middle Cornish onwards. To outlaw such forms or to recommend that they be avoided, can only serve to strengthen the view that revived Cornish is an artificial construct.

There is moreover another reason that *nyng, nynj* cannot be late corruptions. In the later language the distinction between *nyns* in main clauses and *nag* in subordinate clauses has to a large extent been lost. Where Middle Cornish says *nyns eus* 'there is not' the later language has *nag eus, nag es*. This can be seen from the following rather random examples:

ha lebben **nag ez** *buz nebbaz en pow ma* 'and now there are not but a few in the country' NBoson

Nag ez *triuath vêth do vi* 'I do not at all pity' AB: 244c

Nag es *moye vel pager pe pemp en dreau nye ell clappia...* 'There are not more than four or five in our town who can speak...' Bodinar

It follows, therefore, that *nyng, nynj* are Middle Cornish forms of necessity. Late Cornish had largely replaced them with *nag*.

Note that in his dictionaries Nance for 'to reap' correctly cites *myjy*. This agrees with *midzhi* in Lhuyd and *medge* in Pryce, who probably got the word from Thomas Tonkin. Some modern dictionaries, however, cite the word as *mysi, a form which is nowhere attested. *Mysi is an assumption of a variant which should have occurred. Some people may say that it is a reasonable assumption—but the variant has so far not been seen.

3.8 ⟨GH⟩ AS USED IN REVIVED CORNISH ORTHOGRAPHY

The consonant group *gh* has been inserted into spellings in the revived language, although such spellings are poorly attested in the medieval texts, if they are attested at all. Yet, we are told, that the same medieval texts form the basis of the revived language. Such largely unwarranted emendations to the medieval language are not the only ways in which the revived language fails to represent the medieval texts on which it claims to be based. There are many further features of the language which were developing or had already developed and are exemplified in the earliest (late 14th century) texts. Yet some revivalists on hearing such features used by others, condemn them as being from "later and corrupt Cornish." One can only ask: why is the natural development of the language deemed by some to be "corrupt", when it already attested in the earliest texts? It would seem simply to be that such critics are unhappy that the language did not develop along the idealized lines which they themselves desire for the language.

Another regrettable feature of the revived language heard from the lips of Cornish learners is pronunciation of medial ⟨gh⟩. The combination ⟨gh⟩ between vowels and after *r* and *l* is not a feaure of Cornish. It is rather an "aspirational" and etymological spelling, based on a very few examples in the earliest texts. As a result, in the revived languages we have spellings like *byghan (nowhere attested in the texts), *fleghes* 'children' and *arghans* 'silver' (wrongly used to mean 'money'). Although there are examples of the spelling ⟨gh⟩ in the texts, they are not the general rule. Though they are unhesitatingly included in modern dictionaries from Nance's day to the present, in many instances, *they should not be there at all*. The spelling ⟨gh⟩ represents the voiceless velar fricative [x]. Since, however, this sound is absent from English, many Cornish learners substitute the sound closest to it in their own speech. We thus often hear *bikan 'small', *flekes 'children' and *arkans 'silver, *money'. Such pronunciations are the result of an unnecessarily archaizing orthography and make a mockery of the revival's claims to authenticity.

The learners mispronunciation is particularly noticeable in the items *byghan 'small' and *marghak, 'knight', plural *marghogyon. Even Morton Nance, who was renowned for his slavish adherence to his own devised spellng system, had grave doubts about ⟨gh⟩ in *marghak, marghogyon,* etc., as can be seen from his 1938 dictionary, where he writes *mar(gh)ak* 'rider', *mar(gh)oges* 'horsewoman' and *mar(gh)ogeth* 'to ride', that is to say with the *gh* in brackets, as though it could be omitted. In spite of this initial hesitancy, however, in his subsequent dictionaries—and continued in most "modern" dictionaries since Nance's time—these words were, and continue to be, written with *gh*.

There was a period when the current Standard Written Form (SWF) was introduced and words such as *byhan, marhek* were so written, that is to say with ⟨h⟩ rather than ⟨gh⟩. Subsequently the SWF after a number of years was revised to remove any irregularities. At this point the forms with *gh* were reinstated, being considered by the revising authority to be the correct spelling. One can only ask why was this decision made, when the most cursory examination of the Middle Cornish texts would show that spellings with *gh* are unjustified. In all the texts, *byghan* is not found at all. The nearest variant is *beghan* at PA 53c, 166b. Let it not be forgotten that *Pascon agan Arluth* dates from c. 1375 and is thus the earliest long text that we have.

§3.9 COLLOQUIAL DOESN'T MEAN CORRUPT

Everywhere else 'small' is written *byhan*, *byan*, or *bean*, i.e. wihout medial ⟨gh⟩. Listed below are all the examples of the various spellings for the Cornish for 'small' from the texts.

3.9 THE CORNISH FOR 'SMALL' AS SEEN IN THE TEXTS
3.9.1 Forms with -*gh*-
ʒe worte vn lam **beghan** 'from them a small distance' PA 53c
nyng ew ow faynys **beghan** 'my torments are not small' PA 166b

Note that ****byghan*** is not attested anywhere in any Cornish text, yet it was Nance's recommended spelling.

3.9.2 *Byhan, byhen*
my ha'm gurek ha'm flogh byhan 'I and my wife and my small child' OM 397
avel flogh **byhan** *maylys* 'wrapped up like a little child' OM 810
reys yv thy'so lafurrya vn pols **byhan** *alemma* 'you must journey a little distance from here' OM 1268-69
bras ha **byhen** 'great and small' OM 2305
yma thy'mmo yn certan the wruthyl vn pols **byhan** *takclow pryve* 'indeed I have private matters to perform for a small while' PC 90-3.

3.9.3 *Byan, byen*
flogh **byen** *nowyth gynys* 'a little newborn child' OM 806
ha tus **vyan** *ha tus vras* 'both unimportant men and important men' OM 1438
kekyfrys **byan** *ha bras* 'both great and small' OM 1653
kekyffrys **byan** *ha bras* 'both great and small' OM 1695
tormentors bras ha **byan** 'torturers great and small' OM 2682
lemyn ol **byan** *ha bras knoukyough ef del dyndylas* 'now you all small and great strike him as he has deserved' PC 2082-83
en prysners bras ha **byan** 'the prisoners great and small' PC 2250
byan *a bras* 'great and small' PC 2348
ha war agas flehes **vyan** *ken the ole why a's byth* 'and you will have cause to weep for your little children' PC 2643-44
reys yv thy's gyne vn pols **byan** *lafurye* 'you must walk a little way with me' PC 3003-04
mytern yn bryton **vyan** 'a king in Brittany' BM 169
rewlys on brays ha **byan** 'we are governed great and small' BM 257
bras ha **byan** *pub huny* 'great and small, everybody' BM 267
forsakyans **byen** *ha muer teryov trefov an bys ma* 'let small and great forsake lands and farms in this world' BM 384-85

benen gans the flogh **byen** 'woman, with your little child' BM 1550
orth flehys gruergh ha **byen** 'to child innocent and small' BM1692
why hagis flehys **vyan** 'you and your little children' BM 1676
duen alemma verement brays ha **byen** 'let us truly go hence great and small' BM 2927-28
maria the vap **byen** *gene dre yth a hythov* 'Mary, your little son will come home with me today' BM 3629-30
the cresy **byen** *ha brays* 'to believe, small and great' BM 4117.

3.9.4 *Bean, vean*

nag o offence **bean** 'that the offence was not small' TH 4
drehevys war questyon **bean** 'arisen upon a small question' TH 19
An pith ew tra **vean** *the vos gwrys* 'Which is a small thing to be done' TH 24a
mas tra **vean** *ha fawt* **bean** 'only a small matter and a small fault' TH 28a
in kythsame lesson **bean** *cut ma* 'in this same small short lesson' TH 28a
ha nys ens y mas parcell **bean** *a aphrica* 'and they were only a small area of Africa' TH 32
bean *ha brase* 'great and small' CW 118
den in mes **bean** *ha brase* 'let us go out, small and great' CW 2481
'Ma lever **bean** *rebbam* 'I have beside me a little book' NBoson.

3.9.5 *Bian, bian*

An lyzûan **bîan** *ʒen i ar nedhez, ez a tivi en an halou nei, ez kreiez Plêth Maria* 'The small plant with the twisted stalk, which grows on our hills, is called Lady's tresses' AB: 245a
BÎAN 'little'; *coos* **bîan** 'the little wood' Pryce L1.

3.10 THE CORNISH FOR 'SMALL' AS SEEN IN PLACE-NAMES

It is clear that ⟨gh⟩ [x] had been greatly weakened in the spoken language as early as the middle of the thirteenth century. This can be seen from place-names throughout Cornwall. The names are cited as follows: today's name, the parish (in parentheses); the form of the first attestation and the date thereof followed by the etymology of the form in question:

Scarrabine (St Endellion): Roscarrec bian (1249) < *Roscarrek bian* 'little Roscarrock'
Vounder (Mullion): Boundervian (1268) < *bownder vian* 'little droveway'
Trengilley (Constantine): Trekellybyan (1287) < *tre an kelly bian* 'little farm at the grove'
Trenance (Mullion): Trenansbyan (1289) < *tre nans bian* 'little valley farm'

§3.10 COLLOQUIAL DOESN'T MEAN CORRUPT

Tregoose (St Erth): Tregosbyan (1301) < *tre goos bian* 'little wood farm'
Nanspean (Gunwalloe): Nansbyan (1302) < *nans bian* 'little valley'
Bosporthennis (Zennor): Pordhunes vyan (1313) < *porth enys vian* 'little gateway to Ninnes'
Priske (Mullion): Preskebyan (1327) < *prysk bian* 'little brushwood'
Trebiffin (Lesnewth): Trebyan (1327) < *tre bian* 'small farm'
Nanpean (St Stephen in Brannel); Nanspian (1332) < OC *nant pian* 'little valley'
Gothers (St Dennis): Gudefosbian (1334) < *goothfos bian* 'little stream wall'
Landrine (Ladock): Landreynbyan (1338) < *landreyn bian* 'little site of thorns'
Trequite (St Kew): Tregoydbyan (1350) < OC *tre guit bian* 'little wood farm'
Trevean (Morva): Trevian (1356) < *tre vian* 'little farm'
Trebyan (Lanhydrock): Trebyan (1393) < *tre bian* 'little farm'
Trevean (Newlyn East): Drefvyan (1398) < *an drev vian* 'the little farm'
Penhallick (Illogan): Penhellekbyan (1430) < *pen helyk bian* 'little end of willows'
Cardinham (Crowan): Cardynan Vyan (1430) < *ker dynan vian* 'little fort camp'
Skewes (St Wenn): Skywysbian (1443) < *skewys bian* 'little place of elder trees'
Bosullow (Wendron): Bossewolouvyan (1447) < *bos chy wolow vian* 'little dwelling place at Chywolow'
Polgrain (St Wenn): Polgren Vyan (1449) < *pol greun vian* 'little grain pool'
Treweeg (Stithians): Trewyke Vyan (c.1474) < *tre wig vian* 'little churchtown farm'
Tolgus (Redruth): Talgoys Vian (c.1475) < *tolgoos via*n 'little hole wood'
Trevine (St Minver): Trevyan (c.1495) < *tre vian* 'little farm'.

It is quite apparent from the Cornish texts and from the place-names listed above that the Cornish word for 'small' has been *byan, bian, bean* since the thirteenth century. The form **byghan* preferred by Nance is entirely without warrant. 'Small' in Cornish should be written *byan* or *bian* according to the orthography preferred. There is no justification for a spelling *byghan*. Not only would *byan, bian* be closer to the traditional language, it would also avoid the spurious pronunciations *['bixən] and *['bikən].

3.11 'HORSEMAN, KNIGHT' AND 'TO RIDE' IN CORNISH

Nance after 1938 spelt 'knight, horseman' as *marghak* and his plural was *marghogyon*. He also spelt the verbal noun 'to ride' as *marghogeth*. None of these spellings with ⟨gh⟩ is found anywhere in the texts. The attested forms are as follows:

3.11.1 'Knight, horseman'

gans peswar **marreg** *a brys* 'by four important knights' PA 190b

ȝe bub **marreg** *ran nayse* 'for every knight a share ?' PA 190b

vn **marreg** *longis hynwys* 'a knight named Longinus' PA 217a

ȝen **marreg** *worth y hanow y a yrhys may whane* 'they commanded the knight by name that he should pierce' PA 218b

peswar **marrek** *yrvys ens* 'they were four armed knights' PA 241d

Pan deȝens y bys yn beth yȝ eth vn **marrek** *ȝy ben* 'When they came to the tomb one knight approached his head' PA 242b

Pan o pur holergh an gyth y tefenas vn **marrek** 'When the day was very late one knight awoke' PA 244a

En **marrek** *na a sevys oll yn ban y goweȝe* 'That knight aroused all his companions' PA 245a

Marrak *aral a gowsas* 'Another knight spoke' PA 246a

kefrys **marrek** *ha squyer* 'both knight and squire' OM 2004

vrry ov **marrek** *guella my a vynsa the pysy* 'Uriah, my best of knights, I would entreat you' OM 2139-40

ha del oma **marrek** *len benythe ny thof an plen* 'and as I am a loyal knight, never shall I come from the field' OM 2150-51

my a'd pys may fy asper avel marrek fyn yrvys 'I besech you that you be savage as a finely armed knight' OM 2203-04

saw vn **marrek** *a'n lathas ha the'n dor scon a'n goras* 'but a knight killed him and quickly brought him to the ground' OM 2226-27

vrry nep o **marrek** *len* 'Uriah, who was a loyal knight' OM 2338

ov bolnogeth purguir yv rag gorthia crist galosek bones sacris **marrek** *du* 'my wish indeed is in order worship mighty Christ to be consecrated a knight of God' BM 348-50

Plos **marrek** *pour dar seposia prest a reta omma settya orth emperour* 'You utterly base knight, what, do you indeed presume here to oppose an emperor?' BM 2444-47

Elider eth of hynwys, the Arthor **marrak** *gostlys* 'I am called Elider, a knight plighted to Arthur' BK 1513-14

noble **marrak**, *me a grys, ny ombrevys in dan scoys* 'a nobler knight, I believe, never proved himself under a shield' BK 1632-33

§3.11.2 COLLOQUIAL DOESN'T MEAN CORRUPT

Marrak *lym orth both ow brys, uhal-worthyys of i'n bys* 'A harsh knight as my mind desires, I am highly respected in the world' BK1648-49

marrack *en pedden west pow Densher* 'a knight in the west of Devonshire' NBoson.

It should be noted, however, that Lhuyd, presumably using written sources, cites both *Marhag* AB: 57a and *Marhak* AB: 240c.

3.11.2 'Knights, horsemen'

dun alemma **marrouggyon** 'let us go hence, knights' OM 1639

marregyon *me agas pys* 'knights, I beseech you' PC 1613

marregyon *heil heil thywhy* 'knights, hail, hail to you' PC 2347

eugh lemmyn ow **marreggyon** 'go now, my knights' RD 361

out warnough fals **marregion** 'curses on you, treacherous knights' RD 607

marregyon *theugh ny won blam* 'knights, to you I ascribe no blame' RD 657

dukis ʒurlys **marogyon** 'dukes, earls, knights' BM 294

an keth tra na **marrogyon** *parusugh wy* 'that same thing do you prepare, knights' BM 220-21

Duen ny in kerth gans mur a nerth ov **marogyon** 'Let us go away with much force, my knights' BM 813-15

genevy a fur termyn **marogyen** *duen alema* 'with me shortly, knights, let us go hence' BM 1741-42

dugh gena ow **marogyon** 'come with me, my knights' BM 4359

Marrogyon *flowr, wylcum o'm tyr* 'Choice knights, welcome to my country' BK 1946

Marrogyan, *leverugh why pan worshyp…* 'Knights, declare what compensation…'

prynsys, dukys, **marrogyon** 'princes, dukes, knights' BK 2381

I o chyf ow **marogyon** 'They were my chief knights' BK 2385

3.11.3 'To ride' (verbal noun)

my a vyn athysempys **marogeth** *ware bys ty* 'I will immediately ride soon thither' OM 1970-71

marogeth *my ny alla yma cleves y'm body* 'I cannot ride, there is sickness in my body' OM 2145-46

nyng ew guyw the **vorogath** 'he is not worthy to ride out' BK 929

nyng ew guew the **varogath** 'he is not worthy to ride out' BK 3227.

3.12 THE CORNISH FOR 'CHILDREN' IN THE TEXTS

Nance wrote *flogh* 'child' and *fleghes* 'children'. Following him the SWF writes *fleghes*. The evidence of the texts, however, suggests that *flehes* would be a more authentic spelling.

3.12.1 *Fleghas, fleghes,* etc. with medial *-gh-*

*hag ynweth agan **fleghys*** 'and also our children' PA 246c
*yn mesk **fleghys** ysrael* 'among the children of Israel' OM 1553
*an benenes ha'n **fleghys*** 'the women and the children' OM 1575
*tus benenes ha **fleghys*** 'men, women and children' OM 1588
*tus benenes ha **fleghys*** 'men, women and children' OM 1611
fleghes ebbrow dvn yn vn rew 'Hebrew children, let us go in a line' PC 239
*ihesu pendra leuerta a'n **fleghys** vs ow cane* 'Jesus, what do say of the children who are singing?' PC 431-32
*a ganow a'n **fleghys** da* 'from the mouths of good children' PC 437
*hag ynweth war y **fleghas*** 'and also upon his children' PC 1924
*pur wyr y tue vyngeans tyn mar pyth an guyryon dyswrys warnough war agas **fleghys*** 'very truly bitter vengeance will come, if the just man is destroyed, upon you, upon your children' PC 1937-39
*drok thu'm **fleghys** na duan* 'harm to my children nor affliction' PC 1945
*y tue uyngeans war the wour ha war the **fleghys** keffrys* 'vengeance will come upon your husband and upon your children also' PC 1949-50
*ha war y **fleghys** keffrys* 'and upon his children also' PC 1964
*ha war the **fleghys** keffrys* 'and upon your children also' PC 2201
*may hallons ynno bewa ha'gha **fleghys** bynytha* 'that they might live in it and their children forever' PC 2833-34
*ha war ol agan **fleghas*** 'and upon all our children' PC 2503
*ynweth the ol ow **fleghes*** 'also to all my children' RD 162
*lemman warbarth ow **fleghys** ow bennath thywhy pupprys* 'now together, my children, my blessing to you always' RD 306.

3.12.2 *Flehas, flehes, flehys* with medial *-h-*

*mar te venions ha cothe war agan **flehys*** 'if vengeance happen to fall upon our children' PA 149cd
***flehys** mur ha benenas* 'great children and women' PA 168c
*ha'y wrek ha'y **flehes** kefrys* 'and his wife and his children also' OM 932
*kemer the wrek ha'th **flehas*** 'take your wife and your children' OM 975
*sav vnsol ty ha'th **flehas*** 'except only for you and your children' OM 1031
*ha'y wrek ha'y **flehes** kefrys* 'both his wife and his children also' OM 1035
*the wrek ha'th **flehas** kefrys* 'your wife and your children' OM 1159

§3.12.2 COLLOQUIAL DOESN'T MEAN CORRUPT

*my ha'm gurek ha'm **flehas*** 'me and my wife and my children' OM 116
*ha'm gurek ha'm **flehes** kefrys* 'both my wife and my children also' OM 1258
*tus benenes ha **flehys*** 'men, women and children' OM 1623
*ha war agas **flehes** vyan* 'and upon your little children' PC 2643
*may fenygough an torrow na's teve bythqueth **flehes*** 'that you may bless the wombs that never bore children' PC 2646-47
*hag y3 yv marthys densa sur worth **flehys*** 'and he is wonderfully kind indeed to children' BM 40-1
*se3ovg mereasek yn myske an **flehys** pur dek* 'sit, Meriasek, very nicely among the children' BM 93-94
***flehys** yonk a gar boys* 'young children like food' BM 116
*drys oll **flehys** an pow ma* 'above all children of this land' BM 183
*lues den eff re lathays ha **flehys** prest in pov ma* 'many men he has killed and children indeed in this country' BM 1118-19
*Lemen warbarth ov **flehys** ny a vyn moys alemma* 'Now together, my children, we shall go hence' BM 1321-22
***flehys** pur reys yv dyugh fest the kuntel dres ol an pov* 'it is very necessary for you to collect children throughout the country' BM 1507-08
*me re ruk **flehys** ievvje rag astevery an coel* 'I have made children, I tell you, to make up the loss' BM 1589
*mar mennyth oma latha **flehys** bythqueth na pehes* 'if you wish here to kill children that never sinned' BM 1592-93
*Pysul yv sum an **flehys*** 'What is the total of the children?' BM 1604
*poys yv gena dyswuthel heb ken an keth **flehys** ma* 'I am reluctant to destroy these same children without a cause' BM 1633-34
*Regh an **flehys** thage mam* 'Give the children to their mothers' BM 1667
*ha then **flehys** delles da* 'and to the children fine clothes' BM 1674
*why hagis **flehys** vyan* 'you and your little children' BM 1676
*dren pyte a gemeras orth **flehys** gruergh ha byen* 'by the pity you showed to children innocent and small' BM 1691-92
*rag na scollyas goys an **flehas*** 'since he did not shed the children's blood' BM 1698-99
*drefen kemeres pyta an **flehys** gruegh del rusta* 'because of the pity you took on the innocent children' BM 1704-05
*bath may rellen in vr na in goys tum an **flehys** na* 'that I might then take a bath in the warm blood of those children' BM 1777-78
*mur trueth y kemerys latha prest kemys **flehas*** 'much pity I felt in killing so many children' BM 1781-82
*rag the pyte a gemercys an **flehys*** 'because of the pity you took on the children' BM 1836-37

*ny wothogh why ov **flehes** pendryv ol boys an ena* 'you do not know my children what is all the food of the soul' BM 2014-15

*Ov **flehys** wek eugh why dre* 'My dear children, go home' BM 2676

*Ov **flehys** eugh why de dre* 'My children, go you home' BM 3149

*cresugh helma ov **flehas*** 'believe this, my children' BM 3153

*maria nu'm bus **flehys** marnes vn map* 'Mary, I have not children but one son' BM 3192-93

*bethens ov gol vy nefra sensys gans ov **flehys** dour* 'let my festival be held exactly by my children' BM 4322-23

*ov **flehys** gruegh y gutha in hanov du* 'my children, cover him in the name of God' BM 4542-43

*ha'm mam ha'm **flehys** inweth* 'both my mother and my children also' BK 1552

*Rag henna, ow **flehys**, gesow ny the vos war a re an par na* 'Therefore, my children, let us be ware of people like that' TH 9

*an **flehas** a thespleasure han wroth a thu* 'the children of displeasure and the wrath of God' TH 10a

*orth agan gylwall ny an **flehes** a thesplesians* 'calling us the children of displeasure' TH 7a

*may hallow why bos **flehes** agys tas vsy in neff* 'that you may be children of your Father who is in heaven' TH 22

*mar tha ragan, ys an tas a neff thegan reputya hagan kemeras ny rag y **flehes*** 'as good for us as the Father of heaven to acknowledge us and to take us for his children' TH 22a

*an **flehis** a thu* 'the children of God' TH 23a

*theworth **flehis** an teball ell* 'from the children of the devil' TH 23a

*an re na neb ew an **flehis** a thu* 'those who are the children of God' TH 24

*fatell one ny **flehis** agan tas vs in neff* 'that we are children of our Father who is in heaven' TH 26

*na gweras a **flehes*** 'nor the assistance of children' TH 28

*ow **flehes**, merow war agys bewnans* 'my children, examine your life' TH 28a

*cowse an beseth an **flehis*** 'talk of the baptism of children' TH 37

*an re na a throlla an **flehis** the vos besitthis* 'those who would bring the children to be baptized' TH 37a

*kepar hay **flehis** kernsyak* 'like his loving children' TH 41

*kepar ha **flehes** ow shackya gans pub waffe* 'like children shaking with every gust' TH 42

*may teffa pub naturall mam ha maga y **flehes** gans an substans ay corfe* 'that every natural mother may nurture her children with the substance of her body' TH 54a

§3.13   COLLOQUIAL DOESN'T MEAN CORRUPT

*lowarth mamb wore e **flehis** the benenas erall* 'many mothers send their children to other women' SA 59
*why a vyth avell **flehys*** 'you shall be like children' CW 653
*thymo ve ha thom **flehys*** 'to me and to my children' CW 1035
*rag gule dillas thom cutha ha thom **flehys** es genys* 'to make clothes to cover me and for my children who have been born' CW 1038-39
***flehys** evall ha gentell* 'obedient and gentle children' CW 1061
*hagen **flehis** kekeffrys* 'and our children also' CW 1385
*ha vij plag te hath **flehys** a vyth plagys* 'and with seven plagues you and your children shall be afflicted' CW 1614-15
***flehys** am bes denethys* 'if have begotten children' CW 1979
*na skydnya an keth vengeans in neb termyn warnan ny nagen **flehys*** 'lest the same vengeance fall at any time upon us nor upon our children' CW 2208-10
*hay wreag hay **flehys** keffrys* 'both his wife and his children also' CW 2227
*ha tha wreag ha tha **flehys*** 'both your wife and your children' CW 2252
*rag ow sawya haw **flehys*** 'to save me and my children' CW 2311
*keffrys ow gwreak haw **flehys*** 'both my wife and my children' CW 2374
*Kewgh abervath ow **flehys*** 'Enter in, my children' CW 2436
*thethe wreag hathe **flehys** keffrys* 'your wife and your children also' CW 2476
*menas noy y wreag hay **flehys*** 'except Noah, his wife and his children' CW 2540.

3.13 THE CORNISH FOR 'KIND, KINDRED; UTMOST'

Nance wrote *eghen* 'sort, kind' and the SWF follows him. The evidence of the texts, however, suggests that *ehen* would be a more authentic spelling:

3.13.1 Eghen

*mara pe a'n keth **eghen** o dyfynnys orthyn ny* 'if it was of the same sort that was prohibited to us' OM 211-12
*aspy yn ta pup **eghen** whythyr pup tra ol bysy* 'examine well every sort; search everything thoroughly OM 747-48
*a bub **eghen** best yn wlas* 'of every kind of animal in the land' OM 977
*A bub **eghen** a kunda gorow ha benow yn weth* 'Of every kind male and female also' OM 989-90
*yn dyspyt ol th'y **eghen*** 'in spite of his utmost' PC 1010
*me a'n clewas ov tyffen na vo reys awos **heghen** trubit vyth the syr cesar* 'I heard him forbidding that no tribute for any consideration be given to Sir Caesar' PC 1573-75
*re wruk the vohosugyon sawye pup **eghen** clefyon* 'he healed for the poor every kind of sick person' PC 3108.

3.13.2 *Ehen*

*ȝe thu ny goth thys temptye yn neb **ehan** a seruys* 'your God you should not tempt in any kind of service' PA 15ab

*Ha spycis leas **ehen*** 'And spices of many sorts' PA 236a

*bost a wrens tyn ha deveth yn gweȝens worth y **ehen*** 'they were making a sharp and shameless boast that they would keep him in spite of his utmost' PA 242d

*meth vyth ol d'agen **ehen*** 'it will be shame to all our kin' OM 2066

*the voth prest yn pup **hehen** y goulenwel yv ow whans* 'to perform your will in every respect indeed is my desire' PC 1091-92

*yn dyspyt th'aga **hehen*** 'in spite of their utmost' PC 2527

*me a geneugh yn lowen mar callen guthyl **hehen** a socor nag a seruys* 'I will go willingly with you if I can perform any sort of succour or assistance' PC 3006-08

*wy yv pen agen **ehen*** 'you are the head of our kindred' BM 318

*nyns yv worschyp theth **ehen*** 'it is no honour to our kin' BM 360

*neb yv pen ol y **ehen*** 'who is the head of all his kindred' BM 1159

*ha les the oll y **ehen*** 'and advantage to all his kindred' BM 2913

*Nyng ew repref tho'm **ehan*** 'There is no reproof to my kindred' BK 96

*accontys an gwelha gowr us a'm **ehan** hethew bew* 'he is considered the best man of my kin who is alive today' BK 2494

*place delicyous dres **ehan*** 'a place delicious beyond everything' CW 361

*lower flowrys a bub **ehan*** 'many flowers of every sort' CW 363

*ha coole orthaf os **ehan*** 'and harken to me at all costs' CW 595

*a bub **ehan** a gynda* 'of every kind of sort' CW 2270

*ha lavonowe pub **ehan*** 'and ropes of every kind' CW 2291

*a bub **ehan** a vestas drewhy quick ȝym orthe copplow* 'of every kind of animal bring quickly to me in pairs' CW 2411-12

*ha sacryfice lebmyn radn **ehan** a bub sortowe* 'and sacrifice now some share of all kinds' CW 2487-88

*pub **ehan** ha beast in byes* 'every sspecies and animal in the world' CW 2512.

3.14 THE CORNISH FOR 'EVENING'

This word is attested once in OCV; there are four instances only of it in the Middle Cornish texts; there are several more examples in the later language. In none of them is medial *-gh-* written. Nance, in spite of his preference for medieval forms, did not write the word with *-gh-*, not even in his later dictionaries, since he always prefers to write *gorthewer*. The SWF initually wrote *gorthuher*; it now follows some other forms of revived Cornish with spelling *gorthugher. This spelling is wholly unattested. So one can only

§3.14.1   COLLOQUIAL DOESN'T MEAN CORRUPT

ask what possible warrant is there for the spelling *gorthugher and where did it come from?

3.14.1 *Gorthugher with medial -gh-
There are no examples.

3.14.2 Gorthuwher without medial -gh-
gurthuwer 'vesperum' [evening] OCV
rak namnag yw **gorthuer** 'for it is almost evening' RD 1304
bys yn newer **gorȝewar** 'until yesterday evening' BM 103
rag **gurthuhar** *ha myttyn nyng es thenny mar tha car* 'for evening and morning we have not such a good friend' BK 827-28
gurthuherow *ha myttyn* 'in the evenings and in the morning' BK 2744
an **gothihuar** *ha metten* 'the evening and morning' JBoson, BF: 51
gethihuer *ha metten vo nessa jorna* 'evening and morning were the second day' JBoson, BF: 52
Ha **gethihuer** *ha metten o an tridga jorna* 'And evening and morning were the third day' JBoson, BF:
Ha **gethiuar** *ha mettin o an padgurra jorna* 'And evening and morning were the fourth day' JBoson, BF: 52
Ha **gethihuer** *ha mettin o an pempas jorna* 'And evening and morning were the fifth day' JBoson, BF: 52
ha **gethihuar** *ha mettin ve an veffras jorna* 'and evening and morning were the sixth day' JBoson, BF: 53
gydhihuar 'crepusculum' [dusk] AB: 52b
gydhiu̯har 'hesperus' [the evening star] AB: 65b
Mi vedn ȝyz guelaz arta **ȝydhyhu̯ar** 'I'll see you again in the evening' AB: 244c.

Regrettably the greeting *gorthugher da* often pronounced *gorthuger da*. A week medial *h* or *wh* is perhaps to be allowed in these words, but to write them with *gh* pronounced [g] is wholly unacceptable. KS has normalized -*uw*-, -*u*-, -*ew*-, -*uh*-, -*ihu*-, -*iu*-, -*iu̯h*-, and -*yhu̯*- and writes *gordhuwher* with a variant *godhuwher*.

3.15 THE SPELLING OF THE WORD FOR 'SILVER'
The word *arhans* in Cornish means 'silver', though it is frequently misused to mean 'money' (see 6.1 below).

3.15.1 Arghans
owr hag **arghans** *gwels ha gweth* 'gold and silver, grass and trees' PA 16b
an **arghans** *a gemeras* 'he took the silver' PA 103b.

3.15.2 *Arhans*

fenten bryght avel **arhans** 'a spring as bright as silver' OM 771

my a vyn bos garlont gureys a **arhans** *adro thethe* 'I wish that a garland of silver be made around them' OM 2097

saw vn pren gans garlontow a **arhans** *adro thotho* 'but one tree with garlands of silver around it' OM 2500

an **arhans** *kettep dyner me a's deghes war an luer* 'of the silver every coin I throw them on the floor' PC 1514

en **arhans** *me a gymer* 'the silver I shall take' PC 1537

awos cost **arhans** *nag our greugh y tenne mes a'n dour* 'in spite of the cost of silver or gold do you pull it out of the water' RD 2231-32.

3.15.3 *Arans*

a **arans** *pur ha fyn gurys* 'made of silver pure and fine' OM 2100

An pelle **arrance** *ma ve resse* 'This silver ball was given' TBoson, BF: 38.

The spelling *arghans* is attested in *Pascon agan Arluth* and was adopted by Nance for Unified Cornish. *Arhans* is found more frequently than *arghans*. The occasional spelling without either *-gh-* or *-h-* indicates that the medial segment was simply [r]. *Arhans* has the merit of avoiding the consonant group *-rgh-*. Since the sound of *-gh-* is [x] in Cornish, a sound not found in spoken English, many learners substitute the nearest sound in their own speech. As a result they pronounce the Cornish for 'silver' as **arkans*. In order to avoid such a mispronunciation, the word should be spelt *arhans*.

3.16 THE VERB 'TO FETCH, TO BRING'
3.16.1 *Kerghes*

an asen a ve **kerghys** 'the ass was fetched' PA 28b

hagh ol **kerghys** *dotho th'y wlas* 'and all brought to him in his kingdom' PC 29

kerghys *the'n nef golow* 'brought to bright heaven' PC 79

thywhy ef a vyth **kerghys** 'he will be brought to you' PC 1786

yv the henna y fuen ny ow **kerghas** *an guas thywhy* 'is it for that that we are fetching the fellow to you?' RD 1823-24

whet **kerghough** *thy'mmo pilat* 'bring Pilate to me once more' RD 1885

thu'm gothfos mur dewolow rak y **kerghes** *ef lemmyn* 'to my knowledge many devils in order to fetch him now' RD 2299-300

me agas peys the **kerghas** *gans y enef* 'I beseech you to fetch him with his soul' RD 2308-09.

3.16.2 *Kerhes*

En prynner a veu **kerhys** 'The timbers were fetched' PA 153a
hag anotho a **gerhas** *y eneff 3e dewolgow* 'and from it fetched his soul to darkness' PA 106d
dun th'y **gerhes** *cowethe* 'let's go to fetch him, comrades' PC 2555
th'y **gerhas** *the dre certan* 'to bring it home indeed' OM 2565
the **gerhas** *an guas muscok* 'to fetch the deranged fellow' PC 961
mones certen thy **gerhes** 'to go certainly to fetch it' BM 660
nyns yv awos drokcoleth yth ogh **kerhys** *dymo vy* 'it is not for an evil deed that you have been fetched to me' BM 1768-69
the **kerhes** *dyn meryasek* 'to fetch Meriasek to us' BM 2795
ha mar tuff thagis **kerheys** 'and if I come to fetch you' BM 3365
me as **kerhes** *pur guir de* 'I fetched them very truly yesterday' BM 3410
the **kerhes** *thymo pur clour oma eneff meryasek* 'to fetch to me very gently Meriasek's soul hither' BM 4332.

3.16.2 *Keres*

kerugh *ihesu thy'nny ny* 'fetch Jesus to us' PC 1359.

As can be seen, the spelling of the verb 'to fetch' in Cornish is similar to that of *arhans* 'silver'. The commonest spelling has *-rh-*. And a rarer spelling without either *-gh-* or *-h-* is also found. The spelling in standardized Cornish should be *kerhes*.

3.17 LOSS OF FINAL ⟨GH⟩

Final *-gh* is usually pronounced in revived Cornish in such words as *flogh* 'child', *whegh* 'six', *sëgh* 'dry' and so on. It is apparent, however, that the final consonant, written ⟨gh⟩ and pronounced [x] was being lost in the spoken language at an early date.

The loss of ⟨gh⟩ [x] is also noticeable in the following spellings from the texts:

3.17.1 *Whe* 'six'

ragh y fue kyns y vos gurys dew vgens blythen ha **whe** 'for there were forty-six years before it was finished' PC 350-51

The variant ⟨whegh⟩ is not found in the Middle Cornish texts.

3.17.2 *Saw* 'load'

Ow yowke ve ew wheg, ha ow **sawe** *ew scaff* 'My yoke is sweet and my burden is light' TH 27a

Ny dalle deez perna kinnis war an **sawe** 'You should not purchase firewood by the load' JJenkins

The spelling ⟨sawgh⟩ is not attested.

3.17.3 *Bê* 'burden, load'
yma gene vn **bê** *da* 'I have a good load' OM 1056.

The spelling ⟨begh⟩ is not attested.

The loss of final *-gh-* can also be seen from the following place-names. The modern name and parish are cited first; then the earliest attestation without final *-gh-*; finally the etymological form and meaning are given:

Chyvarloe (Gunwalloe): Tywarlo (1235) < *chy war logh* 'house on the estuary'
East Looe (St Martin-by-Looe): Lo (1237) < *logh* 'deep water, estuary'
Portlooe (Talland) Portlo (c.1250): < *porth logh* 'deep water cove'
Looe (the River); Loo (1298) < *logh* 'deep water'
Kellybray (Stoke Climsland): Kellibre (c. 1286) < *kelly bregh* 'dappled grove'
Loe Bar (Sithney): La Loo (1338) < *logh* 'deep water'.

Although *whe* 'six', *saw* 'load' and *bê* 'burden, load' are all unattested in the texts with final *-gh-*, the three items should in revived Cornish be spelt *whegh, sawgh* and *begh* respectively. The attested word for 'sixth' is *whefes* OM 49 and *wheffaz* John Keigwin. The ordinal *whefes, wheffes* is from *wheghves, where the final [x] of *whegh has been reduced to [h] and has devoiced the following [v] to [f]. This is evidence that the simplex was *whegh at an early stage. The word *saw* 'load' is a congener of Welsh *sawch* 'heap, load' and in Cornish almost certainly ended in *-gh* at one time. It is probably better, however, to use the etymological spelling *sawgh than a form without final *-gh*, in order to distinguish the word from the adjective *saw* 'safe', the conjunction *saw* 'but', and the imperative verb *saw!* 'save!, heal!' *Begh 'burden' is to be recommended as the spelling in the revived language, since the derived verb *beghya* 'to burden' is attested in the second person singular imperative and clearly has a final *-gh*: *saw na* **byhgh** *y war nep cor* 'but do not oppress them in any way' OM 122.

Although *whegh, sawgh,* and *begh* can be recommended as normalized spellings, it should not be forgotten that none of the three words appears

§3.18 COLLOQUIAL DOESN'T MEAN CORRUPT

with final -*gh* in the texts. It is therefore correct to pronounce all three without a final consonant.

3.18 THE LOSS OF ⟨TH⟩ AFTER ⟨R⟩

Apart from the omissions of unstressed particles, the most common omissions in speech—and these are reflected in place names—are the sounds represented in modern spelling by the groups ⟨th⟩ and ⟨dh⟩, or, in phonetic representation, [θ] and [ð] respectively. The medieval scribes had no way to distinguish the voiced member of this pair, i.e. [ð], the sound in **th**is, **th**at, ba**th**e, and smoo**th**, from the voiceless member [θ], heard, for example, in **th**ick, **th**in, **m**o**th**, and sou**th**. In the texts, therefore, both sounds were written ⟨th⟩, as indeed is the case in modern English.

If the ⟨th⟩ or the ⟨dh⟩ occurs medially between two vowels or after *r*, or finally, it is often lost, that is to say, it is not pronounced. This loss is referred to by Jenner in his Handbook as 'apocopation'. Strictly speaking, however, apocopation refers only to the loss of the consonant in final position. Here we will simply refer to the phenomenon as loss of medial and final *th/dh*. Instances of the medial loss of *th/dh* can be seen in *wodhya* > *woya* imperfect of *godhvos* 'to know', for example in Rowe's *an gie oyah teler an gye en noath* 'they knew that they were naked' Gen. iii. 7.

While examples of such loss in final position are to be noted in items like *forth* 'road', *porth* 'harbour', *in kerth* 'away', *abarth* 'on behalf of', the omission of *th* and *dh* can be observed in place-names, for example, *Henvor* < *Henfordh*. Listen also to the local pronunciations of *Pralla* for *Porthallow*, *Prowstock* for *Porthoustock* and *Crinnack* for *Carwythenack*. Final *th* is lost in speech in at least one place-name. In Nancegollan there is the road name *An Vownder Goth*. This was always pronounced by the locals as *Vande Go*.

The reduction of the cluster *rdh* [rð] internally can be seen in the following:

3.18.1 *Kerras* for *kerthes* 'to walk'
tha adam **kerras** *pur greyf me a vyn the sallugye* 'I'll walk very vigorously to Adam to greet him' CW 720-21
in for may wruge eave **kerras** 'in the way that he walked' CW 1767
angye a glowhas leaufe an Arleth Deew a kerras en looar 'they heard the voice of the Lord God walking in the garden' Rowe, Gen. iii.8
Dho **garras** 'Gradior' [walk] AB: 64a.

3.18.2 *In ker* for *in kerdh* 'away'
ke **in ker** *eva benynvas* 'go thou away, Eve goodwife' CW 712
quicke **in ker** *ke alebma* 'quickly go away hence' CW 1208

*rag nang ew hy pryes yn ten mathew res **in ker** vaggya* 'for now it is quite time to travel away' CW 1334-35

*moer vyth nyng eʒa defry the doen **in ker*** 'there was not any sea indeed to carry her away' CW 2426-27

*nyedge **in ker** lemyn ha myer* 'fly away now and look' CW 2451.

3.19 THE PHONETICS OF *R* < *RDH* AND *R* < *RTH*

Although it is not apparent from the spelling, there was probably a phonetic difference between *r* or *rr* as a result of the loss of [ð] in the cluster [rð] and *r* or *rr* as a result of the loss of [rθ], also written ⟨rth⟩. In the cluster [rθ] the second element was voiceless. That is to say that the consonant was produced in the mouth by the tongue and teeth, but without any vibration of the vocal chords. In the group [rð], on the other hand the tongue and teeth produced the sound, but at the same time the vocal chords were vibrating. In other words [rð] was voiced, but [rθ] was voiceless. The consonant [r] is usually voiced. This means that when the second element in [rð] was lost, the ensuing [r] remained voiced. When the second element in the group [rθ] was lost, the [r] itself, which was already voiceless in anticipation of the following voiceless [θ], remained voiceless. The resulting sound was probably form the acoustic point of view [rh] or [r̥]. Cornish orthography had no way of distinguishing the voiced *r* [r] from the unvoiced one [r̥]. There are good reasons, however, for believing that the *r* from *rdh* was not the same as the *r* from *rth*.

3.20 MEDIAL -*RTH*- REDUCED TO -*R*-, -*RR*-

Let us now look at some items containing historic voiceless *rth* reduced to *rr* or *r*:

3.20.1 *Gortheby* 'to answer' > *gorreby*

*an venyn a **worrebys** hag a leverys* 'the woman answered and said' TH 3a

*Jhesus an **gorrybys** hag a leverys thotha* 'Jesus answered him and said' TH 20a

*Eff a **worrebys** fatel essa eff ow supposya...* 'He answered that he supposed...' TH 29

*nena Symon pedyr a rug **gurryby*** 'then Simon Peter answered' TH 44

*ha te a **worryb** Amen* 'and you answer: Amen' SA 61a

***gorrybowhe** oll pub onyn* 'do you all answer every one' CW 143

*ow **gweryby** vskys gwra* 'answer me quickly' CW 1145

*ha venen a **worebaz*** 'and the woman answered' Rowe, Gen. iii.13

*Buz e **gwerebaz** ha lavarraz* 'But he answered and said' Rowe, Matt. iv.4.

§3.20.2 COLLOQUIAL DOESN'T MEAN CORRUPT

3.20.2 *Gorryb* for *gorthyp* 'answer'

me a re thewgh **gurryb** 'I will give you an answer' TH 13a

The hemma yma **gorrub** *pleyn the vos res* 'There is a plain answer to be given to this' TH 24a

tha ***orybe*** *gee* 'your answer' SA 62

hemma yth ew **gorryb** *skave* 'this is a frivolous answer' CW 1198

na thowt **gorryb** *ty a vyth* 'fear not you shall have an answer' CW 1735

hag y teaf thewhy arta gans **gorryb** *kyns es hethy* 'and I will come to you with an answer before ceasing' CW 1760-61.

3.20.3 *Marrojyon* for *marthojyon* 'wonders'

gwra **marvgian** *pan vosta devethis in ban* 'marvel when you have come up' TH 63a

hemma yth ew **marrudgyan** *bras* 'that is a great wonder' CW 2124

an **marodgyan** *es ena* 'the wonders that are there' CW 1804

me a vyn sure y thysca an **marogyan** *dell ew braes* 'I will surely inform him of the wonders how great they are' CW 1875-76

yn paradice y whelys defrans **marodgyan** *heb dowt* 'without doubt I saw various wonders' CW 1897-98

an **marudgyan** *a'go terman* 'the wonders of their time' ACB E e 3v.

From the instances listed above it is apparent that the loss of *th* after *r* in *gortheby* 'to answer' and *marthojyon* 'wonders' has been in Cornish since Tregear's day, i.e. c. 1555. It is neither a late nor a corrupt development.

3.21 FINAL *-GH* WRITTEN AS ⟨TH⟩

It has regularly been claimed that the shift of /x/ to /θ/ occurred only in the Late Cornish period, that is to say in the seventeenth and eighteenth centuries. This view cannot be sustained since there are examples of the change in place-names as early as the thirteenth century. Examples of ⟨th⟩ for ⟨gh⟩ include *Goonamarth* (St Mewan) < *gun an margh* 'the horse's down' from 1542 and *Ventonveth* (Veryan) < *fenten vergh* 'the horses' well' from 1545. The name *Lannarth* (Lannarth) is from *lanergh* 'clearing' and exhibits final ⟨th⟩. The earliest attestation of the name is from 1413 where it appears as *Lannargh*.

The same apparent shift of ⟨gh⟩ > ⟨th⟩ can also be seen in Tregear's homilies and in the *Creation of the World* in the following instances:

y vab po y **virth** 'his son or his daughter' TH 21a (*virth* is for *vyrgh* 'daughter)

LANGUAGE CHANGE §3.21.1

nyns esa na **marth**, *charet, na army* 'there was neither horse, chariot nor army' TH 56a (*marth* is for *margh* 'horse')
maga whyn avell an **yrth** 'as white as snow' TH 56a (*yrth* is for *ergh* 'snow').
marth *ha casak hag asan* 'stallion and mare and ass' CW 406 (*marth* is for *margh* 'horse').

When final -rth was weakened to [rh] or [r̥], it would have been from the acoustic point of view virtually identical with -*rgh*, i.e. [rx] weakened to [rh]. As a result some confusion appears to have occurred. Scribes were not sure whether final [rh] should be written ⟨rgh⟩ or ⟨rth⟩. At all events that the confusion in spelling between final ⟨gh⟩ and ⟨th⟩ is by no means a late and corrupt phenomenon, for it is attested in Tregear's homilies, well inside the Middle Cornish period.

By far the commonest instance of this apparent shift of final -*rgh* > -*rth* can be seen in the word *warlergh* 'after, according to'. Examples of *warlerth*, *warlyrth* are numerous. Here are some examples from the texts:

3.21.1 *Warlerth* 'after, according to' for *warlergh*

kowses **warlerth** *an maner an bobill* 'spoken according to the manner of the people' TH 1

kewses **warlerth** *an maner an bobyll* 'spoken according to the manner of the people' TH 1

warlerth *an examplys a dus tha* 'according to the examples of good men' TH 10

Walkyow ha gwandrow **warlyrth** *an spuris* 'Walk and wander according to the Spirit' TH 16a

fatell res thyn scripture bos vnderstondyys **warlerth** *an generall menyng a egglos crist* 'that the scripture must be understood according to the general sense of the Church of Christ' TH 18

So not **warlerth** *an priveth interpretacion a then vith* 'But not according to the private interpretation of any man' TH 18

neb na garra y gyscristian **warlyrth** *an kyth sort ma* 'who does not love his fellow Christian according to this sense' TH 20a

Warlerth *y vynd hay appetyd y honyn* 'According to his own mind and appetite' TH 21

hag yth esans ow pewa **warlerth** *an letterall sens a la moyses* 'and they were living according to the literal sense of the law of Moses' TH 26a

Ha the whelas ha gylwall **warlyrth** *gyvyans ha pardon* 'And to seek and to call after forgiveness and pardon' TH 30a

warlerth *aga mynd aga honyn* 'according to their own mind' TH 33

§3.22 COLLOQUIAL DOESN'T MEAN CORRUPT

fatell rug agan saviour Jhesus crist cowse the abosteleth **warlyrth** *an vaner ma* 'that our Saviour Jesus Christ spoke to the apostles according to this manner' TH 35a

na rellan ny **warlyrth** *agan fantasy agan honyn iudgia an dra* 'that we should not judge the matter according to our own imagination' TH 37

warlyrth *an measure an lene oys a crist* 'according to the measure of the complete age of Christ' TH 42

rag eff a recevyas Corf Dew **warlerth** *badd maner* 'for he received the Body of Christ according to an evil way' SA 65a

Ow amor, denvenough why etho **warlerth** *arlythy* 'My love, do you therefore send after lords' BK 3012-13

mes pub eare ma ow crya **warlerth** *an oyle a vercy* 'but at all times does he call after the oil of mercy' CW 1795-96

in vr na gwaytyans dewhans **warlerth** *oyle mercy pub pryes* 'at that time let him immediately wait for the oil of mercy always' CW 1863-64.

It is clear that *warlerth* for *warlergh* is by no means a corrupt form of Late Cornish. It is an integral part of Middle Cornish of the sixteenth century.

It also appears that final *-gh* when reduced to [h] was understood to be a reduced variant of ⟨th⟩ [θ]. Speakers therefore on occasion confused the two. This accounts for modern forms like *Polzeath* < *pol segh* 'dry pool'.

3.22 LOSS OF FINAL ⟨TH⟩ [Θ] AFTER A VOWEL

It is also noteworthy that the final segment *th* [θ] in the word *meneth* 'mountain' is frequently lost, and at an early date. The following attestations of place-names in *meneth* + second element indicate just how common was this loss. Here are cited the contemporary name followed by the parish, then the date of its earliest attestation followed with loss of final segment, and last of all the etymological form and translation:

Luxulian (Luxulian): Menedu (1200) < *meneth du* 'dark hillside'
Minnimeer (Tremaine): Menamur, Menmer (1201) < *meneth meur* 'great hillside'
Menacuddle (St Austell): Menaquidal (1251) < *meneth cuidel* 'hillside with a small wood'
Menadue (Tintagel): Menadu (1290) < *meneth du* 'dark hillside'
Menadue (St Breward): Menedieu (1356) < *meneth du* 'dark hillside'.

The final segment in the word *meneth* 'mountain, hill' is also lost in absolute final position. This can also be seen from place-names:

Trewarmenna (Creed): Trewarmene (1282) < *tre war meneth* 'farm on a hillside'
Menna (St Dennis): Mene (1302) < *meneth* 'hill, hilside'
Penmennor (Stithians): Penmene (1321) < *pen meneth* 'top of hillside'
Trevenna (St Mawgan): Trewarvene (1327) < *tre war veneth* 'farm on a hillside'
Trewarveneth (Paul): Trewarvene (1345) < *tre war veneth* 'farm on a hillside'.

Compare also Glasney (Budock): Glasney (1284) < *glasneth* 'verdure'.

3.23 INITIAL MUTATIONS

Mutations of initial consonants are an important aspect of Cornish, as indeed of all the other Celtic languages, and cannot therefore be dismissed. Many are those who believe that a missed mutation is a catastrophe. This happens very frequently, for example, when a speaker of the revived language does not know that a noun is feminine, and thus fails to lenite the initial consonant after the article. It must be admitted, however, that initial mutations were frequently omitted in the Middle Cornish texts themselves. This does not, of course, mean that the scribes did not know where mutations were required, but rather that they did not trouble to show them in writing. In *Pascon agan Arluth* there are many unmarked mutations. These 'missed' mutations in *Pascon Agan Arluth* are as follows (the expected mutated form is given in parentheses):

*en bys pan **d**eyskynnas (**th**eyskynnas)* 5b
*gull penans ef a **p**esys (**b**esys)* 10b
*An ioul a **t**rylyas (a **d**rylyas) spery* 18a
*y demptye pan **p**rederis (pan **b**rederis)* 19b
*vn pres yn geyth na **p**eghy (na **b**eghy)* 20c
*ȝe **p**edyr (**b**edyr) crist a yrghys* 72a
*In vrna y a **c**olmas (**g**olmas)* 76a
*Gans henna ef a **c**lewas (**g**lewas)* 86a
*ȝoȝo bys pan **d**anvonas (**th**anvonas)* 87d
*mars os du del **d**anvansys (**th**anvansys)* 93b
*cafas daffar pur **p**arys (**b**arys)* 105d
*ef a thueth a **g**alyle (alyle)* 107c
*bos Ihesus a **g**alyle (a alyle)* 108a
*pylat bys pan **d**anvonas (**th**anvonas)* 110c
*war **d**yth pasch worth an Iustis (war **th**yth)* 124c
*ȝe **c**reatur ny vye (ȝe **g**reatur)* 151b

§3.24 COLLOQUIAL DOESN'T MEAN CORRUPT

*ʒe **p**ur **t**reytours y ʒewle (ʒe **b**ur **d**reytours)* 157a
*En debell wrek **c**asadow (wrek **g**asadow)* 159a
*Vn venyn **d**a a welas (venyn tha)* 177a
*pan esa yn **c**rows pren (**g**rows pren)* 183d
*ʒe **c**rist (**g**rist) may fe crehyllys* 184d
*na gans oll y **t**retury (**d**retury)* 194d
*annoʒo dell **d**everas (dell **th**everas)* 221c
*a rug may **w**rellons (**wh**rellons) terry* 229c
*Pan **d**eʒens (**th**eʒens) y bys yn beth* 242a
*del **d**eth an nef wary fyth (del **th**eth)* 244b
*Pan **d**eʒons (ʒethons) ʒe alyle* 258a.

3.24 ABSENCE OF INITIAL MUTATION IN PLACE-NAMES

As far as Cornish place-names are concerned, it seems at times that they follow their own rules. Frequently in toponyms expected mutations do not occur. On the other hand on occasion initial mutations are shown when they are wholly unexpected. For example, the parish name *Tremaine* never exhibits a mutated form. As early as *c.* 1150 the initial *m* remains unmutated. Furthermore the variant *Tremayne*, attested in St Gennys, Crowan and St Columb Major has unmutated *m* and has done so throughout the centuries.

Many users of revived Cornish in our day believe that place-names with the first element *tre f.* + a second element beginning with *m-*, should by rights be spelt and pronounced with an initial *v*. Yet it is quite clear, that although some revivalists do indeed lenite the initial *m* in *Tremail, Tremar, Tremeer, Tremethick* and *Tremewan*, for example, there is no historical warrant for such lenition. If native speakers in former times used such names without muating the initial consonant of the second element, modern revivalists would be well advised to follow suit and leave the initial *m* unmutated.

Any form to be used as a spelling in the revived language should not seek to correct. It is best to adhere to the historical form for each name. If mutation did occur, even if once only, then it could be argued that it is probably legitimate to mutate now. If lenition did not occur when we think that it ought to have done, because the form appears to violate our rules, the sensible approach is to leave the name alone. There was obviously some reason in those days why in these instances mutation was not effected, which we do not understand. It is not legitimate to assume that a mutation was forgotten or missed, for there are many place-names exhibiting lack of expected mutation. There are so many names without expected mutation that we cannot ascribe them all to error. With all our modern expertise, there are aspects of Cornish which are not yet fully understood.

Another anomaly involves the presence of *p* in place-names as an apparent mutated form of *b*. Thus the name *Nanpean* occurs in the parishes of St Stephen-in-Brannel, St Just in Penwith and Stithians. It seems that the original name in the Old Cornish period was *Nant byghan. Here the final *t* being voiceless appears to have devoiced the contiguous *b* > *p*, giving *Nantpyghan. Then the *t* was lost from the consonant cluster to give *Nanpyan, *Nanpean*, the attested form. The form *Nanspean* in Gunwalloe and St Enoder is best explained as a reshaped variant of *Nanpean*. Cornish speakers in the Middle Cornish period, knew that *nans* meant 'valley', and thus replaced the unfamiliar form *nan-* in this name with the more recognizable form *nans*.

A further example of initial *b* appearing as *p* is can be seen in place-names. The basic form *Porthbean* is found in St Keverne, Gerrans and St Anthony in Roseland. In St Austell however as early as early as 1337 we find the form *Porthpean*, although an earlier *Porthbean* is also attested. It would seem that in St Austell, though not elsewhere, the voiceless cluster *-rth-* devoiced initial *b* in the second element in *Porthbyan to *Porthpyan, *Porthpean*. Since native speakers of Cornish pronounced the name as *Porthbyan, *Porthbean in some places and as *Porthpyan*, *Porthpean* in another, modern revivalists should follow their example and write *Porthbyan*, *Porthbian* in one case and *Porthpyan*, *Porthpian* in the other.

3.25 RHOTACIZATION OR THE SHIFT OF [Z] > [R]

Another phonetic change occurring in the later development of Cornish was the change of ⟨s⟩ to ⟨r⟩. This was not universal but applied particularly to *gasa* 'to let, to allow' which changed to *gara* and above all to *yth esof* 'I am', etc. and *yth esa* 'was', etc. which changed to *theram* and *thera* respectively. The earliest examples seem to be in Tregear (*c.* 1555) and *Sacrament an Alter* (*c.* 1560):

> *rag mar pethans* **gerys** *the vois* 'for if they are allowed to escape' TH 25a
> *rag neg* **eran** *cregy nanyle regardia gerryow Dew* 'for we neither believe nor heed the words of God' SA 59
> *Neg* **eranny** *ow kemeras hemma rag common bara ha dewas* 'We do not take this for common bread and drink' SA 63a
> *an bara* **erany** *ow tyrry* 'the bread which we break' SA 65.

Thera for *yth esa* became virtually the *only* way in which this was spelt, another natural development but which is apparently unacceptable nowadays.

3.26 PRE-OCCLUSION

Pre-occlusion refers to the phenomenon seen in some Cornish texts in which after a stressed short vowel *n* is preceded by a furtive and unexploded *d* (e.g. *penn* 'head' > *pedn*; *henna* 'this' > *hedna*), while *m* similar circumstances is preceded by an unexploded *b* (*mamm* 'mother' > *mabm*; *lemmyn* 'now' > *lebmyn*). In the later texts in disyllables the pre-occluded part of the cluster begins to dominate the whole, while the sonant portion is entirely eclipsed. Thus *hedna* becomes *hedda*, and *lebmyn* becomes *lebbyn*.

Pre-occlusion, it seems, is something that is either liked or abhorred. It cannot be denied, however, that it is part of the natural development of Cornish. Again it is not purely a facet of Late Cornish, as it appears in a few instances in the later Middle Cornish texts. There are three examples of *bedneth* 'blessing' in *Beunans Meriasek* (written in 1504), at lines 198, 224 and 225. The next occurrence is probably Borde's *me a **vyden** gewel* 'I will do' from 1547. There are no examples in the Cornish of John Tregear, although the text is very long indeed. The spelling *mamb* 'mother' in *Sacrament an Alter*, folio 59 seems to be an instance of pre-occluded *m*. In William Jordan's *Creation of the World* from 1611, pre-occlusion is common.

Pre-occlusion where reluctantly tolerated in modern standardized Cornish should only be used, according to the language authorities, by those speakers and writers from West Cornwall, because that is where it started, and was never found anywhere towards the East. There is much in this argument; since pre-occlusion is found in place-names in the Scilly Isles where Cornish became extinct in the early sixteenth century, but is not found in Tregear, vicar of Newlyn East, in the 1550s. It is to be remarked, however, that Nance based much of the sound system of Unified Cornish on Lhuyd's description, but he avoids the use of pre-occlusion, even though it is a noticeable feature of Lhuyd's Cornish. The presence or absence, however, is from the sixteenth century onwards not a question of chronology but of dialect. *Beunans Meriasek* is older than Tregear's Homilies and exhibits three examples of pre-occlusion. Tregear's Homilies in spite of their length have no instances. The much shorter text *Sacrament an Alter* seems to have one example (*mamb* 'mother'). Clearly chronology is not the decisive factor. Pre-occlusion of *n* is a function of the maintenance of a distinction between a lenis or short /n/ and its fortis or long counterpart /ṇ/. Dialects which maintained the distinction between /n/ and /ṇ/, pre-occlude /ṇ/ to /dn/. Those dialects in which /ṇ/ and /n/ fall together as /n/, do not. In these non-pre-occluding dialects, however, in order to keep utterances apart, the vowel preceding the lenis /n/ was, where possible, lowered; thus *e* became *a*. This explains why, for example, the pre-occluded form *bedneth* 'blessing' has [e] as the stressed vowel, but the form without pre-occlusion is always *banneth*. *Banneth is never pre-occluded; there is no *badneth anywhere in Cornish. This same distinction will also explain Lhuyd's Cornish forms s.v. *Iste* 'this, that, he', i.e. *Hana* and *hedda* (AB: 73b). *Hana* and *hedda* both represent spoken forms of *henna* 'that, that man, he'. The pre-occluded form has *e*; the form without pre-occlusion has the lowered vowel *a*. Again pre-occlusion versus no pre-occlusion is a question of dialect, not chronology.

3.27 PRE-OCCLUSION IN THE 16TH AND 17TH CENTURIES

3.27.1 *Beunans Meriasek* (1504)
bedneth *ȝyvgh* 'blessing to you' 198
bedneth *crist* 'the blessing of Christ' 224
bedneth *ȝe vam* 'thy mother's blessing' 225

3.27.2 Andrew Borde (1547)
me a **vyden** *gewel ages commaundement why* 'I will do your commandment'

3.27.3 *Sacrament an Alter* (c. 1560)
lowarth **mamb** 'many mothers' SA 59

3.27.4 Richard Carew (1602)
Tedna 'Draw' 26
march **guiddan** 'white horse' 127
ednack 'eleven' 127
Pedn *joll* 'Devil's head' 127
Pedn mouzack 'Stinking head' 127
Meea na **vidna** *cowza sawzneck* 'I can speak no Saxonage' 127
Omdidna 'Shrinking' 217.

3.27.5 *Creation of the World* (1611)
in **idn** *dewges* 'in one godhead' 6
vdn *dew* 'one God' 11
pan **vidnaf** *ve comanndya* 'when I will command' 36
ha bos **pedn** *in nef* 'and be chief in heaven' 82
war y **bydn** 'against him' 440
udn *eal wheake* 'a sweet angel' 759
theth **pedn** *ȝagy* 'thy head' 916
yskydnyow *eall splan* 'descend, you bright angel' 964
pedn *cowge* 'dolt head' 1090
y vaw ny **vidna** *boos* 'I will not be his servant' 1154

§3.27.5 COLLOQUIAL DOESN'T MEAN CORRUPT

*frute da **bydnar** re thocka* 'may it never bear good fruit' 1161
*der tha **wadn** ober* 'by thy evil deed' 1275
*me as kyef pan **vydnaf** ve* 'I get them whenever I want' 1457
*gans gwaracke **tedna*** 'to shoot with a bow' 1466
*na a veast na **lodn** in beyse* 'nor of beast or bullock in the world' 1471
*na gwyne ny vsyan **badna*** 'nor wine do we use a drop' 1474
*y **bedna** ʒym ny vyn ef* 'his blessing to me he will not' 1541
*un **lodn** pur vras* 'a very large bullock' 1546
*henna o **gwadn** ober gwryes* 'that was an evil deed done' 1679
*ny **vidn** ef gava* 'he will not forgive' 1694
*squattys ew tha **ampydnyan*** 'smashed are your brains' 1705
*haw **fedn** squatyes* 'and my head crushed' 1707
*my a **vydn** gwella gallaf* 'I will the best I can' 1710
*ty a gyef in yet **vdn** eall* 'you will find an angel at the gate' 1753
*ha serpent vnhy **avadn*** 'and a serpent in her above' 1809
*debbry an avall a ankan o **defednys*** 'to eat the apple of sorrow which was forbidden' 1813-14
*pan vo pymp myell ha pymp cans a **vlethydnyow** clere passhes* 'when five thousand and five hundred years have clearly passed' 1861-62
*a **vlethydnyowe** moy es cans* 'more than a hundred years' 1915
*hag a **vydn** the vayntaynya* 'and will support you' 1950
***vdn** spyes* 'a while' 1969
*Sevys a **lydnyathe** pur vras* 'Sprung from a very great lineage' 2097
*ioies nef in **vdn** rew* 'the joys of heaven in a row' 2145
*lemyn me es goer in **badn*** 'now I will put them up' 2202
*na **skydnya** an keth vengeans* 'lest the same vengeance fall' 2208
*rag cola orthe **vdn** venyn* 'for harkening to a woman' 2213
*kynth ota **skydnys** in wharthe* 'though you have collapsed in laughter' 2306
*te **pedn** pylles* 'you bald head' 2318
*tha **radn** an ry na* 'to part of those' 2356
*a **skydn** warnough* 'shall fall upon you' 2369
*rag dew a **vydn** danven lywe* 'for God will send a flood' 2370
*y **fydn** dew gwill indella* 'God will thus do' 2380
*a **vlethydnyow** pur leas* 'of years very many' 2404
*noy teake te a wore **hedna*** 'fair Noah, you know that' 2447
*does ny **vydnas** an vrane vras* 'the raven would not come 2464
*ethyn bestas ha pub **lodn*** 'birds, beasts and every bullock' 2477
*te a weras **gwadn** ha creaf* 'you helped weak and strong' 2479
***radn** ehan a bub sortowe* 'some king of all sorts' 2488
*ha rag **hedna** gwren ny cana* 'and therefore let us sing' 2491
*rag **hedna** sure me a wra* 'therefore I shall surely make' 2498

*ha rag **hedna** cressowgh* 'and therefore increase' 2509-10
*me a **vidn** ye requyrya* 'I shall require it' 2520
*ny a **vidn** gwyll indella* 'we will do so' 2527
*ny ve **udn** mabe dean sparys* 'not one human being was spared' 2539.

3.27.6 Richard Brome (1632)
***Peden** bras vidne whee bis cregas* 'Bighead, do you want to be hanged?'

3.27.7 Richard Symonds (1644)
idnac 'eleven'

3.27.8 Wella Rowe (c. 1680)
Genesis 3
lebben 'now' 1
radn 'part' 6
radne 'part' 6
aprodnieo 'aprons' 7
pedn 'head' 15
*Ve **vedn** goerah zoer* 'I will put anger' 16
leben 'now' 22
*Rag **hedda*** 'Therefore' 23.

Matthew 2
leben 'now' 1
*e a **vednas** (< ev a wovydnas)* 'he asked' 4
*e a **vednyas** (< ev a wovydnas)* 'he asked' 7
***kebar** (< kebmer)* 'take'
***vedn** whelaz* 'will seek' 13
*me **vedn** crya a mâb* 'I will call my son' 15
*en **dadn** deaw vloth* 'under two years' 16
***kebar** (<* kebmer) *an flô yonk* 'take the young child' 20.

Matthew 4
***bedn** mean* 'against a stone' 6
*ve **vedn** ry theeze* 'I will give you' 9
Leben 'Now' 12
*me **vedn** gee[l]* 'I will make' 19.

Ten Commandments
*en **dadn** en oare* 'under the earth' 2
*compoza **cabmwith'e** sira* 'visit the iniquity of the father' 2

bednath 'blessing' 2
na **vedn** an Arleth 'the Lord will not' 3
bedn ta contrevack 'against your neighbour' 9.

4
DUALS AND PLURALS

4.1 UNATTESTED DUALS IN REVIVED CORNISH
Modern teachers of Cornish tell students to use the dual form rather than the plural for all relevant body parts that come in pairs. Apart, however, from the absence of evidence for many duals, it is apparent that in the later stages of Cornish, the use of duals for those body parts which *did* originally have such forms, was diminishing in frequency. In the Middle Cornish texts, *dewlagas* is slightly commoner than *lagasow*.

Recent research indicates that it was a distinct trend even in the early language for the dual to be replaced by the plural. In particular it is significant that no dual is attested for any of the following: *scovarn* 'ear', *garr* 'leg', *gwews* 'lip', *gwelv* 'lip', *abrans* 'eyebrow', *bogh* 'cheek', *pedren* 'buttock, haunch', and *mordhos* 'thigh'. Indeed dual forms of any of those used in the revived language are inventions The plural *morȝosow (mordhosow)* 'thighs' is early, since it occurs in the phrase *aga morȝosow whare* in *Pascon agan Arluth* 229d.

In the case of some body parts, e.g. *ufern* 'ankle' and *gwewen* for example, no plural form is attested anywhere, although they must have existed in some form. Earlier *troos* 'foot' has one or two attested dual forms, but the plural *treys* is common. On the other hand *leuw* 'hand' did retain its dual form in *dywla* and indeed in later Middle and Late Cornish *dywla* functions as the plural of *dorn* 'fist' with the secondary meaning 'hand'. When 'feet and hands' are spoken about the Cornish phrase is always *treys ha dewla*, i.e. with a plural followed by a dual. This is exactly the same as in Welsh, where 'feet and hands' are rendered *traed a dwylo*. It seems that the dual form *dewdros* fell out of use very early, since the word occurs once only in *Pascon agan Arluth*, whereas in the same document the plural *treys* occurs twice.

Curiously the current word *tron* for 'nose' is unattested. Pryce in his *Archæologia Cornu-Britannica* (much of which was borrowed directly from Thomas Tonkin) cites *tron* as 'nose', but the source used by Pryce or Tonkin is unknown. The ordinary word for 'nose' in the texts is either the dual

§4.2   COLLOQUIAL DOESN'T MEAN CORRUPT

dewfrik or the plural *frigow*, where the basic element is *frig* 'nostril'. *Tron* 'nose' is found in *Vocabularium Cornicum* of the early twelfth century as *trein*. In his dictionary of 1938 Nance gives *tron* < OC *trein* and by comparison with Welsh *trwyn* 'nose'. In his later English-Cornish Dictionary of 1952, however, under 'nose' he cites *frigow* (UC *frygow*) as his first choice.

4.2 THE CORNISH FOR 'HANDS' IN THE TEXTS
4.2.1 *Dewdhorn* 'hands' (dual)
kychys the ves gans **dywthorn** 'snatched away with both hands' RD 2596.

4.2.2 *Dywla, dewla, dowla* 'hands' (plural)
corf ha pen treys ha **dewle** 'body and head, feet and hands' PA 130d
yn **dewle** *an ij ethow* 'in the hands of the two Jews' PA 131a
y **thewleff** *pylat a wolhas* 'Pilate washed his hands' PA 149a
clevas bras es om **dewleff** *deveȝys* 'a great sickness has come upon my hands' PA 156b
Reys o ȝoȝo dysqueȝas ȝe pur treytours a[n] **ȝewle** 'He was obliged to show the hands to the very traitors' PA 157a
awos bos claffy **ȝewle** 'because his hands are diseased' PA 158b
dre y **ȝewleff** *bys yn pen* 'through his hands right up to his head' PA 178c
ow eneff me a gymyn arluth yn tre ȝe **ȝewle** 'my soul, Lord, I commend into your hands' PA 204d
gew a ve yn y **ȝewle** *gans an eȝewon gorris* 'a spear was put into his hands by the Jews' PA 217c
ȝe **ȝewle** *neb an gwyskis* 'to the hands of him who struck him' PA 219b
ov **dywluef** *colm ha'm garrow* 'bind my hands and my legs' OM 1346
me a vyn mos the vre ow arluth treys ha **devle** 'I will go to anoint my Lord, feet and hands' PC 476
ha'n kelmyns treys ha **dule** 'and let them bind him feet and hands' PC 583
yma ow trys ha'm **dule** *thyworthef ow teglene* 'my feet and my hands are shaking off me' PC 1216-17
ha kelmys treys ha **dule** 'and bound feet and hands' PC 2163
ha treys ha **dyulef** *kelmys* 'and feet and hands bound' PC 2375
me a wolgh scon ow **dule** 'I will straightaway wash my hands' PC 2499
y dreys ha'y **dule** *yn ten gans kentrow worth an plynken bethens tackys* 'and let his feet and his outstretched hands be fixed with nails to the timber' PC 2514-16
rak mar claf yv ow **dule** *ny alla handle toul vyth* 'for my hands are so diseased I cannot handle any tool' PC 2677-78
ha garow yn y **thule** 'and rough in his hands' PC 2733
myserough tol th'y **thule** 'measure a hole for his hands' PC 2740

DUALS AND PLURALS §4.2.2

*pan fo guw yn y **thule** me a hyrgh thotho hertye* 'when there is a spear in his hands I will order him to thrust' PC 2921-22

*treys ha **dyvlef** a pup tu fast tackyes gans kentrow hern* 'feet and hands on both sides firmly fixed with iron nails' PC 2937-38

*a tas yntre the **thule** my a gemmyn ow spyrys* 'Father, into thy hands I commend my spirit' PC 2985-86

*an thyv yn mes a'y **thywle*** 'the two out of his hands' PC 3153

*tel y'th **dyvluef*** 'holes in your hands' PC 3174

*squerdys y treys ha'y **thywle*** 'his hands and feet torn' RD 1265

*hag yn treys hag yn **thyvle*** 'both in the feet and in the hands' RD 1542

*mos the wolhy ow **dule** a thesempes me a vyn* 'I shall go immediately to wash my hands' RD 2202-04

*spygys bras dre ow **dywle*** 'great spikes through my hands' RD 2590

*kentrewys treys ha **dula*** 'nailed feet and hands' BM 2603

*kentrewys gans ʒethewon treys ha **dule** eredy* 'nailed by the Jews feet and hands indeed' BM 2990-91

*treys ha **dule** kentreweys* 'feet and hands nailed' BM 3035

*Y ij **luff** y trehevys* 'He raised his hands' BM 4431

*the vos golhes a **thewleff** du* 'to be washed by God's hands' TH 8

*delyuerans the worth oll drogkoleth a **thewleff** agan tas a neff* 'deliverance from all evil from the hands of our Father in heaven' TH 8a

*spykys bras a horne dre an treys ha **dewlef*** 'great spikes of iron through the feet and hands' TH 15a

*gans agan **dewleff** ha treys* 'with our hands and feet' TH 21a

*penag ull person a rella eff ha gora y **thewleff** warnotha* 'whatever person he might lay his hands upon him' TH 46a

*fatell yllans gwetias favowre a **thewleff** aga thas a neff* 'how can they expect favour from the hands of their Father in heaven?' TH 55a

*vgy intyr **dowla** tws an beis* 'that is in the hands of men of the world' SA 60

*an kigg ew touchis gans **dowla*** 'the flesh is touched by hands' SA 60a

*pan vonsy y recevia ef ha e corf benegas ef gans **dowla** mustethas* 'when they receive him and his body with sullied hands' SA 61

*neb vge o recivia corf Dew gans **dowla** mustethas* 'who receives the body of God with sullied hands' SA 61

*ef a ve degys inter e **thowla*** 'he was brought into his hands' SA 65

*inter **dowla** an pronter* 'into the hands of the priest' SA 66

*poran gans y owne **dewla*** 'with his own hands exactly' CW 1531

*et ago **doola*** 'in their hands' Rowe, Matt. iv.6

4.3 THE CORNISH FOR 'FEET' IN THE TEXTS
4.3.1 *Dewdros* 'feet' (dual)
ij droys Ihesus caradow 'the feet of Jesus, the beloved' PA 159c
hag a'y thewtros kekyffrys 'and from his hands also' PC 3154

4.3.2 *Treys* 'feet' (plural)
pedyr a sconyas ihesus ʒe wolhy y dreys 'Peter refused that Jesus should wash his feet' PA 46a
corf ha pen treys ha dewle 'body and head, feet and hands' PA 130d
rag y dreys y a vynnas telly 'for they wished to pierce his feet' PA 178d
worth y dreys ha worth y ben 'at his feet and at his head' PA 236c
hag arall ʒy dreys ynweth 'and another to his feet also' PA 242b
avel olow age threys 'like the prints of their feet' OM 760
hagh a's set y dan y treys 'and put them under his feet' PC 251
me a vyn mos the vre ow arluth treys ha devle 'I will go to anoint my Lord, feet and hands' PC 473-74
yma daggrow ow klybye the dreys 'tears are wetting your feet' PC 482-83
ha war the treys magata 'and upon your feet also' PC 488
golhy ow treys ny hyrsys 'you did not command my feet to be washed' PC 518
pup vr ol amme thu'm treys 'always kissing my feet' PC 525
ha'n kelmyns treys ha dule 'let them bind him feet and hands' PC 583
golhy mara qureth ow treys 'if you wash my feet' PC 845-46
saw y treys na vons sethys rag gulan yv ol yredy 'but his feet, unless they be bathed, for they are all clean indeed' PC 863
ytho mar kruge golhy agas treys h'aga seghe 'therefore if I washed your feet and dried them' PC 875-76
golhens pup treys y gyle 'let each man wash his fellow's feet' PC 877
yma ow trys ha'm dule thyworthef ow teglene 'my feet and my hands are shaking off me' 1216-17
ha kelmys treys ha dule 'and bound feet and hands' PC 2163
ha treys ha dyulef kelmys 'and feet and hands bound' PC 2375
y dreys ha'y dule yn ten 'his feet and hands stretched out' PC 2516
ny allaf seuel yn fas war ow treys 'I cannot properly stand on my feet' PC 2612-13
ha tol th'y trys hep lettye 'and a hole for his feet without delay' PC 2741
treys ha dyvlef a pup tu 'feet and hands on both sides' PC 2937
ellas bones the treys squerdys 'alas that your feet are torn' PC 3172
syghsys y treys gans the thyvpleth 'you dried his feet with your plaits' RD 854

DUALS AND PLURALS §4.3.3

squerdys y ***treys*** *ha'y thywle* 'his feet and his hands torn' RD 1266
hag yn ***treys*** *hag yn thyvle* 'both in the feet and in the hands' RD 1542
er an ***treys*** *me a'n kylden* 'by the feet I will drag him backwards' RD 2082
garrow ha ***treys*** 'legs and feet' RD 2501
dre ow ***thrys*** *y tuth vn smat gans kentrow* 'a ruffian went through my feet with nails' RD 2587-88
the trettya indan y ***dreys*** 'to be trodden under his feet' BM 2030
indan ov ***threys*** *me as glus* 'under my feet I will make them pulp' BM 2398
kentrewys ***treys*** *ha dula* 'nailed feet and hands' BM 2603
treys *ha dule eredy* 'feet and hands indeed' BM 2991
treys *ha dule kentreweys* 'feet and hands nailed' BM 3035
aga ***threis*** *ew paris rag skollia goos* 'their feet are ready to shed blood' TH 7a
Gesow ny the veras war agan ***treis*** 'Let us look at our feet' TH 9
dre an ***treys*** *ha dewleff* 'through the feet and hands' TH 15a
gans agan dewleff ha ***treys*** 'with our hands and feet' TH 21a
y ben a ve ***treylys*** *thyn dore in crowse ha y dreys in ban* 'his head was turned downward on the cross and his feet upwards' TH 47
gwregh honora scavall e ***dryes*** 'honour the stool of his feet' SA 64a
pandrew an scavall e ***drys*** *eff* 'what is his footstool?' SA 64a
an grond ew an skavall ow ***thrys*** *ve* 'the ground is my footstool' SA 64a
rag honora scavall e ***drys*** 'to honour the his footstool' SA 64a
tha vos noth ***tryes*** *corf ha bregh* 'that you are naked, feet, body and arm' CW 873
ty a weall allow ow ***thryes*** 'you will see the prints of my feet' CW 1748
ma a weall ooll ***tryes*** *ow thas* 'I see the print of my father's feet' CW 1763.

It is noteworthy that in traditional Cornish the customary expression for 'hands and feet' is *treys ha dewla*, literally 'feet and (two) hands', the first element being a plural and the second a dual. The collocation of dual and plural in this phrase is reminiscent of *traed a dwylo* 'feet and hands' in Welsh where there is the same admixture of dual and plural. The following are the examples of the phrase *treys ha dewla* from the Cornish texts:

4.3.3 *Treys ha dewla* 'feet' (plural) and 'hands' (dual)

corf ha pen ***treys ha dewle*** 'body and head, feet and hands' PA 130d
ow arluth ***treys ha devle*** 'my lord, feet and hands' PC 474
ha'n kelmyns ***treys ha dule*** 'and let them bind him feet and hands' PC 583
yma ow ***trys ha'm dule*** *thyworthef ow teglene* 'my feet and hands are shaking off me' PC 1216-17

§4.4 COLLOQUIAL DOESN'T MEAN CORRUPT

ha kelmys **treys ha dule** 'and bound feet and hands' PC 2163
ha **treys ha dyulef** *kelmys* 'and feet and hands bound' PC 2375
y **dreys ha'y dule** *yn ten* 'his feet and his hands stretched out' PC 2516
treys ha dyvlef *a pup tu* 'feet and hands on either side' PC 2937
squerdys y **treys ha'y thywle** 'torn his feet and his hands' RD 1266
hag yn **treys hag yn thyvle** 'both in the feet and in the hands' RD 1542
kentrewys **treys ha dula** 'nailed feet and hands' BM 2603
treys ha dule *eredy* 'feet and hands indeed' BM 2991
treys ha dule *kentreweys* 'feet and hands nailed' BM 3035
spykys bras a horne dre an **treys ha dewleff** 'great spikes of iron through the feet and hands' TH 15aga
gans agan **dewleff ha treys** 'with our hands and feet' TH 21a.

4.4 THE CORNISH FOR 'EYES' IN THE TEXTS
4.4.1 *Dewlagas* 'eyes' (dual)
y scornye hay voxscusy trewe yn y **ʒewlagas** 'mocking him and buffeting him, spitting in his eyes' PA 83b
y wholhas y **ʒewlagas** 'he washed his eyes' PA 219c
hay dagrow a ʒevera hay **dewlagas** 'and her tears were dropping from her eyes' PA 222b
An goys na dagrennow try dre y **ij lagas** *y ʒeth* 'Of that blood three drops came to through her eyes' PA 225a
yn dyspyt thy **thewlagas** 'in spite of his eyes' OM 2058
me a'th pys yn cheryte a sawye ow **dewlagas** 'I beseech you in charity to heal my eyes' PC 395-96
lemyn gans ow **devlagas** *sur me a wel* 'now with my eyes surely I see' PC 410-11
arluth agan **dewlagas** *yv marthys claf ow colyas* 'lord, our eyes are wondrous sick with watching' PC 1066-67
yn dyspyt the'th **devlagas** 'in spite of your eyes' PC 1193
war y fas ha'y **deylagas** 'on his face and eyes' PC 1395
me a tru sur vn clotte bras ware yn y **theulagas** 'I will spit a great clot soon in his eyes' PC 1399-40
the **thevlagas** *a dre dro* 'round about your eyes' PC 2102
ha henna ny a'n guylwyth gans **devlagas** 'and that we shall see with our own eyes' RD 53-4
yn sur gans ow **devlagas** *ow syuel me an guelas* 'surely with my eyes I saw him rising' RD 520-30
me a'n guelas dre mur ras a'n beth gans ov **devlagas** *ow mos the'n nef* 'I saw him by great grace with my eyes going to heaven from the tomb' RD 616-18

*roy thy'm gans ow **dewlagas** y weles wheth* 'may he grant me to see him again with my eyes' RD 791-92
*me tha vo[na]s lethys en ath **dewlaga**[s] lemyn* 'that I should be killed in your two eyes now' CW 1647
Deaulagaz 'The eyes' AB: 242b.

4.4.2 *Lagasow, lagajow* 'eyes' (plural)
*arak agan **lagasow*** 'before our eyes' RD 1492
*hagys **lagasow** a vith clerys* 'and your eyes will be cleared' TH 3a
*teg the sight y **lagasow*** 'fair to the sight of her eyes' TH 3a
*ow dalhe **lagasow** an bobyll* 'dazzling the eyes of the people' TH 19a
*gans agan **lagasow** ha scovornow* 'with our eyes and ears' TH 21a
*syttys therag agan **lagasow*** 'set before our eyes' TH 42
*ow quelas gans aga **lagasow** kyge* 'seeing with our fleshly eyes' TH 56
*na ny'n gwelvith **lagasaw*** 'nor will eyes see him' BK 1975
*E weflow ha'y **lagasow*** 'His lips and his eyes' BK 2330
*in spyt in e **lagasow*** 'in spite of his eyes' BK 2711
*gans tha **lagasowe** alees* 'with your eyes wide open' CW 694
*agoz **lagagow** ra bos geres* 'your eyes will be opened' Rowe, Gen. iii. 5
*der o hi blonk tha'n **lagagow*** 'that it was pleasing to the eyes' Rowe, Gen. iii. 6
***lagagow** angie ve gerres* 'their eyes were opened' Rowe, Gen. iii. 7
*lagas, **lagasaw*** 'eye, eyes' Bod.
lagazo 'eyes' AB: 223
lagadzho 'eyes' AB: 223

4.5 THE CORNISH FOR 'LEGS' IN THE TEXTS
4.5.1 **Dywarr* 'legs' (dual)
There are no examples.

4.5.2 *Garrow* 'legs' (plural)
*y wolhas aga **garrow*** 'he washed their legs' PA 45c
*y **arrow** hay ʒeffregh whek* 'his legs and his dear arms' PA232a
*ow dywluef colm ha'm **garrow*** 'bind my hands and my legs' OM 1436
*avel gos pen ha duscouth **garrow** ha treys* 'like blood, head and shoulders, legs and feet' RD 2500-01
*yagh yv ov corff ham **garrov*** 'healed are my body and my legs' BM 711
*hag a russa dyso oma **garrow** pur trogh* 'and would make for you here legs all broken' BM 3829-31

4.6 THE CORNISH FOR 'EARS' IN THE TEXTS
4.6.1 *Dywscovarn* 'ears' (dual)
There are no examples.

4.6.2 *Scovornow* 'ears' (plural)
*gans dornow thotho war an **scovornow** reugh boxsesow trewysy* 'with fists give him painful blows upon the ears' PC 1360-62
*war an **scovornow** bysy* 'smartly upon the ears' PC 1391
*y a vynsa stoppya aga **scovurnow*** 'they would stop up their ears' TH 19
*gans agan lagasow ha **scovornow*** 'with our eyes and ears' TH 21a
*Me a glowt e **skovornow*** 'I will box his ears' BK 1657
*whath ny glowys **skovernow*** 'no ears ever heard' BK 1917
*skovarn, **skovornow*** 'eare, eares' Bod.

4.7 THE CORNISH FOR 'ARMS' IN THE TEXTS
4.7,1 *Dywvregh* 'arms' (dual)
*In vrna y a colmas y **ʒefregh** fast gans cronow* 'Then they bound his arms fast with thongs' PA 76a
*y arrow hay **ʒeffregh** whek* 'his legs and his dear arms' PA 232b
*mayth yv ov **dyvvregh** terrys* 'so that my arms are broken' OM 688
*kelmeugh warbarth y **thywvreg*** 'tie his arms together' PC 1179
*kyn fe the **thyvvregh** mar bras* 'though your arms be so great' PC 1189
*drou e yntre ow **dywvregh*** 'give him into my arms' PC 3159
*yn grous ha **thywvregh** ales* 'on the cross with his arms outspread' RD 1265
*yma debron thum **ij vregh** mar bel ov boys ov powes* 'there is an itch in my arms from my being at rest so long' BM 1187-88
*Yma debren thov **ij vregh** mar bel bones heb gul pegh* 'there is an itch in my arms from being so long without sinning' BM 3432-33
Dibreh 'The arms' AB: 242b.

4.7.2 *Brehow* 'arms' (plural)
Breihaụ 'arms' AB: 242c
*A **breihoụ*** 'My arms' AB: 244b.

4.8 THE CORNISH FOR 'SHOULDERS' IN THE TEXTS
4.8.1 *Dywscoth* 'shoulders' (dual)
*dreheueugh an gist yv gurys crous war **duscoth** cryst* 'lift the beam that has been made a cross onto the shoulders of Christ' PC 2582-33

*agas **dywscoth** kettep chet hertheugh worty hy ynweth* 'with your shoulders, every fellow, push against it also' PC 3068-69
*avel gos pen ha **duscouth*** 'like blood head and shoulders' RD 2500
Diskodh 'The shoulders' AB 242b.

4.8.2 *Scodhow* 'shoulders' (plural)
skooth, ***skothow*** 'shoulder, shoulders' Bod.

4.9 THE CORNISH FOR 'FISTS, HANDS' IN THE TEXTS
4.9.1 *Dewdhorn* 'fists, hands' (dual)
*teuleugh why agas **dywdorn** war an logol* 'lay your hands upon the coffin' RD 2178-79
*kychys the ves gans **dywthorn*** 'snatched away with both hands' RD 2596

4.9.2 *Dornow* 'fists' (plural)
*ha gans ow **dornow** a'n guryn* 'and with my fists I will grip him' PC 1132
*gans **dornow** thotho war an scovornow reugh boxsesow trewysy* 'with fists give him painful blows upon the ears' PC 1360-62
*gans **dornow** ha guelynny* 'with fists and rods' PC 1390
*eff a ve cuffeys gans **dornow*** 'he was struck with fists' TH 15a
*me a'n dorn gans ow **dornow*** 'I shall box him with my fists' BK 2651.

4.10 THE CORNISH FOR 'KNEES' IN THE TEXTS
4.10.1 *Dewlyn, dowlyn* 'knees' (dual)
*may3 eth war ben y **3ewleyn*** 'so that he went upon his knees' PA 54d
*war ben **dewlyn** pan ese* 'when he was on his knees' PA 58a
*Rag gwander war ben **dowlyn** hy an guelas ow co3e* 'For weakness onto his knees she saw him fall' PA 171c
*War aga **dewlyn** y3 e derag Ihesus re erell* 'Upon their knees others went before Jesus' PA 195a
*Hag y ee 3e ben **dewlyn*** 'And they went upon their knees' PA 196a
*3y ben **dowlyn** y co3as* 'he fell upon his knees' PA 220b
*war ben ov **dewlyn*** 'upon my knees' OM 1196
*war pen the **thewglyn** ysel* 'humbly upon your knees' PC 136
*peb ol war pen y **devglyn*** 'everyone on his knees' PC 247
*war pen **dewlyn*** 'upon my knees' PC 3020
*war ben y **ij lyn** purfeth* 'on his knees perfectly' BM 4456
*ov **ij lyn** ham kyk squerdys* 'my knees and my flesh torn' BM 4192
*war y **thewlyn*** 'upon his knees' BK 514
*war ow **dewglyen** kekeffrys* 'upon my knees as well' CW 188.

§4.10.2   COLLOQUIAL DOESN'T MEAN CORRUPT

4.10.2 *Glinyow* 'knees' (plural)
*guase **glynnyow** ha gueresow* 'a footman [*lit.* knee-servant] and assistants' BK 3307.

4.11 THE CORNISH FOR 'NOSE, NOSTRILS' IN THE TEXTS
4.11.1 *Dewfrik* 'nostrils, nose' (dual)
*bethans gorrys in ye **thywfridg*** 'let them be put into his nostrils' CW 1854
*in tha **thewfreyge*** 'in your nostrils' CW 1933.

4.11.2 *Frigow* 'nostrils, nose' (plural)
*gor dotho nes the **frygov*** 'put your nose near to it' BM 1454
*me an set ryb the **frygov*** 'I will set it by your nose' BM 3399
*in y anow hay **fregowe*** 'in his mouth and nose' CW 2088
***freegaw**, freeg* 'nose, nostrils' Bod.
***Frigaụ** brâz* 'naso' [person with big nose] AB: 97a
Frigaụ 'nasus' [nose] AB: 97a, 295a.

4.12 THE CORNISH FOR 'THIGHS' IN THE TEXTS
4.12.1 **Dywvorthos* 'thighs' (dual)
There are no examples.

4.12.2 *Mordhosow* 'thighs' (plural)
*aga **morȝosow*** 'their thighs' PA 229d

Since there are no attested instances of **dywarr* 'legs', **dywscovarn* 'ears', nor **dywvordhos* 'thighs', there is no reason to introduce such duals into the revived language. Indeed to do so in pursuit of an imagined and idealized form of Cornish would be inauthentic.

5
VERBS

5.1 AUTONOMOUS FORMS OF THE VERB

Nance as the basis of the revived language introduced into Unified Cornish grammatical forms which were obsolescent or obsolete already in the Middle Cornish texts. It seems that this was done in order to maintain his ideal of the purity of the older language. Regrettably both the archaic features themselves and the thinking behind them are still vigorously advocated today.

A good example of such archaic features can be seen in the autonomous form of the verb. In the present-future the autonomous form ends in *-yr* or *-er* and is the equivalent of a passive. The logical subject, however, is not mentioned when an autonomous form is used. The present-future autonomous is seen, for example, for example in *y whelyr* 'is seen, will be seen'. Examination of the Middle Cornish texts, however, indicates that this form of the verb is not common, and by the time of *Beunans Meriasek* it is clearly obsolescent. It does not seem to be attested thereafter.

It is perhaps not without significance that first line of *Origo Mundi* (the first of the three plays of the *Ordinalia* of the beginning of the fifteenth century) is *En tas anef* ***y'm gylwyr*** 'I am called the Father of Heaven' (OM 1). In *Beunans Meriasek* (1504), on the other hand, the first line reads *Me* ***yw gylwys*** *duk bryten* 'I am called the Duke of Brittany'. In this second sentence the autonomous form of the verb *y'm gylwyr* 'I am called' has been replaced by the verb *bos* 'to be' + the verbal adjective, i.e. ***me yw gylwys***.

Probably the earliest instance of an autonomous form of the present-future occurs in the prophecy *In Polsethow* ***y whylyr*** *anethow* 'in Polsethow miracles will be seen' in the cartulary of Glasney College. The prophecy may be as old as the second half of the thirteenth century. Here are the other instances from the early texts:

5.1.1 *Pascon agan Arluth*

Rag y ***hyller*** *ervyre* 'For it is possible to decide' 20a.

§5.1.2   COLLOQUIAL DOESN'T MEAN CORRUPT

5.1.2 *Origo Mundi*

*En tas a nef y'm **gylwyr*** 'I am called the Father of heaven' OM 1

*rag y whyrvyth an tyrmyn drethe may **fether** the wel* 'for the time will come when one will be the better through them' OM 45-6

*ny **yllyr** re the worthe* 'one cannot worship thee too much' OM 1852

*growetheugh ov arlut may **haller** agas cuthe* 'lie down my lord, that you may be covered' OM 19234

*hag annethe crous y **wrer** rag crouse cryst ov map ker* 'and from them a cross shall be made to crucify Christ, my beloved son' OM 1936-37

*my a's gor adro thotho may **haller** govos the wyr ha gueles yn blethen hyr py gymmys hys may teffo* 'I will put it around it that one may know indeed and see in a full year what extent it will grow' OM 2101-04

*chyf guythoryon ol a'n gulas a **wother** the dysmegy* 'the chief builders of all the kingdom that can be discovered' OM 2331-32

*may **haller** age lathye gans corbles* 'so that they may be fastened with corbels' OM 2473

*ov corre tvmbyr yn ban may **haller** aga lathye* 'putting the timber up so that they can be fixed' OM 2479-80

*saw aban na **gefyr** ken* 'but since no other is found' OM 2503

*rag ov keusel yth **eder*** 'for people are saying' OM 2794

*mayth **eder** worth the vlamye* 'so that you are being blamed' OM 2797.

5.1.3 *Passio Christi*

*mester genough ym **gylwyr*** 'I am called master by you' PC 873

*may **haller** ry yfle gras ha knoukye prest tys ha tas* 'so that he may be given mischaunce and be knocked thwick-thwack' PC 2076-77

*drewhy thy'm kettep onan may **haller** aga iugge* 'bring them all to me that they may be judged' PC 2251-52

*py **kefer** pren th'y crousye* 'where will timber be found to crucify him?' PC 2535

*ple **kefyr** dyv grous aral* 'where will two further crosses be found?' PC 2576

*rag y **fynner** mara **kyller** gans paynys mer ow dyswul glan* 'for people wish if they can to destroy me utterly with great torments' PC 2600-02

*mara **keller** y wythe a chy na alla yntre the'n darasow* 'if it is possible to keep him from entering with the doors' PC 3058-60.

5.1.4 *Resurrexio Domini*

*ha mar ny **wrer** y wythe y thyskyblon yn pryve a'n lader yn mes a'n beyth* 'and if he is not guarded his disciples will steal him from the tomb' RD 341-43.

5.1.5 *Bewnans Ke*

a wel corf ny **glowyr** *cous benytha gans tavas kyk* 'of a better person no speech will be heard uttered by a tongue of flesh' BK 1272-73

The Thew ef a ra grasaw, th'e gorf pan **relher** *ankan* 'To God he gives thanks when his body is afflicted' BK 536-37

Plenteth lowr a ylleow rag pub maner annyow heb dowt e **kefyr** *genas* 'More than plenty of cures for every kind of complaint can without doubt be found with you' BK 1138-40

mara **qurer** *e procedya* 'if one is going to proceed with it' BK 1414

mar **qurer** *y woodros* 'if he is threatened' BK 1426

Ef ew an bolta mab den a **gampoller** *gans ganow* 'He is the bravest human being that is mentioned by mouth' BK 2319-20

Ny **gefyr** *agys paraw in dan howl in mor na tyer* 'Your like is not to be found under the sun in sea or on land' BK 2406-07.

5.1.6 *Beunans Meriasek*

y feth sur colonov trogh pan **weller** *age lathe* 'there will be broken hearts surely when their slaughter is seen' BM 1571

byth ny **yller** *y sconya* 'never can it be refused' BM 1754

my an kemer pur lowan mar **mynner** *dym y profia* 'I will receive it very gladly if people want to offer it to me' BM 2880

mar sus treytour byth moy feytour a **vynner** *the dalhenna* 'if there is a traitour, or worse still a swindler, people will be wanting to seize him' BM 3437

menogh y **rer** *y pesy* 'often will he be besought' BM 3440.

After *Beunans Meriasek* (1504) there appear to be no examples. It should be noticed also that the verbs which appear in the autonomous forms are largely auxiliary verbs, e.g. *bos* 'to be', *gul* 'to do', *mynnes* 'to wish', *gallos* 'to be able' as well as *cafos* 'to find, to get', *clewes*, *clowes* 'to hear' , *godhvos* 'to be able' and *gweles* 'to see'. The only exception is *gampoller* in *Bewnans Ke*.

In his dictionary of 1938 Nance suggests *godhyr* 'is known' as the present autonomous of the verb *godhvos* 'to know, to be able'. This form is attested once in *Origo Mundi* where it means 'to be able'. There is no example of the verb in the sense 'to know'. The only instances of the Cornish for 'is known' exhibit the verb *bos* 'to be' and the verbal adjective:

maga ver dell yll **bos gothvethis** *gans du, ew openly gothvethis ha gwelys ynans y* 'as much as can be known by God, is openly known and seen in them' TH 14

§5.2 COLLOQUIAL DOESN'T MEAN CORRUPT

yth ew openly **gothvethis** *in marver dell rug crist promysya an conforter* 'it is openly known as much as Christ promised the Comforter' TH 36.

If, therefore, we are basing our Cornish on anything later than *Beunans Meriasek*, on Tregear, the *Creation of the World* or Rowe, there is no need to use any autonomous forms at all.

5.2 A CONSTRUCTION FOR INDIRECT STATEMENT

Nance recommended two ways in which indirect statement might be expressed, and those two ways are still the only two really recommended today.

The first way is to introduce the indirect statement with the particle y followed by the verb in the appropriate tense: *Ev a leverys* **y whelas** *an mab i'n mor* 'He said that he saw the boy in the sea'. The difficulty here is that one has to be fluent enough to supply the inflected forms of a large number of verbs and **all** the most common ones. Not all speakers have reached this level of fluency.

The second method of expressing indirect speech involves introducing the reported clause with the subject followed by *dhe* and the verbal noun (often rather incorrectly known as the infinitive). In this construction, the verb does not indicate the tense; a factor which make the construction quite popular: *Ev a leverys* **ev dhe weles** *an mab i'n mor* 'He said that he saw the boy in the sea'. Although this second construction is relatively easy, and is preferred by the majority of speakers, it has a serious disadvantage: it does not indicate the tense of the indirect statement, which must be inferred from the context.

There is, however, a third way, which Nance for some reason chose to ignore, though it is found in the earliest texts. This construction uses *dell* 'as' followed immediately by the verb, as in English: *Vn venyn da a welas* **dell o Ihesus dystrippijs** 'a good woman saw that Jesus was stripped' *(Pascon agan Arluth* 177a*)*. That quotation is as early as *c*. 1375, yet Nance ignored such syntax, and it is still being ignored today. Why? It is a perfectly sound construction and easy to use.

The same construction is also found using *fatell*, which is usually translated as 'how' in English. *Fatell*, however, very often has the meaning of 'that' and with *dell* with the same sense, is found throughout the Middle Cornish texts. Here are some examples of both *dell* and *fatell* to introduce indirect speech:

5.2.1 Indirect speech with *del*

*par del won lauaraff ʒys intre du ha pehadur acordh **del ve** kemerys* 'as best I can I will tell you that an agreement was made between God and the sinner' PA 8ab

*lemmyn ny a yll gwelas lauar du maga **del ra** neb a vynno y glewas* 'now we can see that the word of God nurtures all who wish to hear it' PA 12cd

*ʒen eʒewan dyrryvys **del o** y fynas synsy* 'he informed the Jews that it was his wish to seize [him]' PA 62c

*Vn venyn da a welas **dell o** Ihesus dystrippijs* 'A good woman saw that Jesus was stripped' PA 177a

*Mam Ihesus marya wyn herdhya an gyw pan welas yn y mab yn tenewyn dre an golon may resas ha ʒen dor an goys han lyn annoʒo **dell deveras*** 'The mother of Jesus, Blessed Mary, when she saw the spear thrust into her son into his side so that it pierced the heart and that the blood and water dropped from him' PA 221a-c.

5.2.2 Indirect speech with *fatel*

*...yv gans ow thraytor dyskis **fatel dons** thov hemeres* 'men have been taught by my betrayer that they come to take me' PA 61cd.

*a tus vas why re welas **fatel formyas** dev an tas nef ha nor war lergh y vrys* 'good people you have seen that God the Father created heaven and earth according to his intention OM 2825-26

***fatel fue** cryst mertheryys rak kerenge tus an beys why a welas yn tyen* 'that Christ was martyred for the sake of the men of the world you have seen completely' PC 3220-22

*ny a fyn leuerel ol yn pow sur the pub den ol **fatel wrussyn** ny keusel orth an arluth ker ihesu* 'we will tell everywhere in the land that we have spoken to the beloved lord Jesus' RD 1339-42

*Arluth me ages guarnyas **fatel** ese turant brays er agis pyn drehevys* 'Lord, I warned you that a great tyrant had risen up against you' BM 3444-46

*yma crist ow promysya ha ow assurya thyn, **fatell** vsy eff worth agan cara ny ha **fatell** one ny flehis agan tas vs in neff* 'Christ promises and assures us that he loves us and that we are children of our Father who is in heaven' TH 26.

It is noteworthy that in Tregear's Homilies, sermons that were intended to be heard by the congregation rather than read by them, the usual way of introducing indirect statement is with *fatell*.

There is a place of course for all three constructions in conversational Cornish. In spite of Nance and current teaching, however, it must be admitted that the third choice, i.e. introducing indirect speech with *dell* or

§5.3   COLLOQUIAL DOESN'T MEAN CORRUPT

fatell is not from the much-maligned later era but attested in the texts from the late fourteenth century onwards. Again one is compelled to ask: Why was it ignored by Nance and why is it *still* ignored today?

5.3 PERSONAL FORMS OF THE VERBAL NOUN *BOS* 'TO BE'

As has been noted, indirect speech can be expressed by use of the verbal noun. A further aspect of this usage involves the verbal noun of the verb *bos* 'to be'. In the texts from an early period *bos* is personalized by means of an enclitic pronoun. Examples of such forms are attested as early as the Ordinalia, e.g. *my a leuerys thywhy* **ow bosa** *henna deffry* 'I have told you that I am that man indeed' PC 1119-20. There are examples also in *Beunans Meriasek* and *Bewnans Ke*. In the *Creation of the World* one finds *ow bosaf* where the enclitic *-af* derives from the first person singular of verbs: *me a vyn may fo gwellys* **ow bosaf** *dew heb parow* 'I wish that it should be seen that I am God without equal' CW 78-9. Later in the same text we read: *ha gwrear a oll an beyse* **y bosta** *Arluth heb pare* 'and Creator of all the world, that you are a peerless Lord' CW 1415-16. In this second case the personalization is for the second person singular.

This construction is also found for other persons—not only in the indirect statement but also where the syntax demands the verbal noun, for example, after *drefen* 'because, since': *Rag ty ny vethys dowtyes* **drefan y bosta** *mar deke* 'For you will not be feared since you are so beautiful' CW 523-24. There are examples of this construction also in the *Tregear Homilies*.

Here are some examples of the construction listed according to the relevant person and number:

5.3.1 1st person: *bosa, bosaf, bosama*

my a leuerys thywhy **ow bosa** *henna deffry* 'I told you that I am he indeed' PC 1119-20

ny gar den ry thym guely podrethek am esely drefen purguir **ov bosa** 'no man wishes to give me a bed because in very truth I am ulcered in my limbs' BM 3060-62

ov sclandra mar mynnogh why ha leferel **ov bosa** *omma cruel why an prenvyth du in test* 'if you wish to vilify me and say here that I am cruel, you will pay for it, as God is my witness' BM 3747-50

tovlel a rons warna vy bones an causer defry begythys rag **ov bosa** 'they throw it upon me that I am the cause indeed because I am baptized' BM 4000-02

Me a wothya, parda! the vota ow recordya **ow bosa** *den eredie* 'I knew by God, that you were making known that I was aman indeed' BK 351-53

VERBS §5.3.3

me a vyn may fo gwellys **ow bosaf** *dew heb parow* 'I wish that it be seen that I am peerless God' CW 78-9;

Cresowh **ow bosaf** *prince creif* 'Believe that I am a mighty prince' CW 116

why a wore yn ta henna **ow bosaf** *gwell es an tase* 'you know that well that I am better than the Father' CW 123

henna degowhe destynye **om bosof** *prynce pur gloryous* 'of that bear witness that I am a glorious prince' CW 127-28

splanna es an howle deverye why a yll warbarthe gwelas **ow bosaf** *sertayn pub preyse* 'more brilliant than the sun indeed you can together see that I am certainly always' CW 132-33

splanna es an tase deffry henna cresowhe **om bosaf** 'more brilliant than the Father indeed that do you believe me to be' CW 225

keffrys me ham cowetha der gletha a vyn trea **ow bosaf** *moy worthya agis an tase* 'likewise I and my comrades by the sword will try whether I am more worthy than the Father' CW 316-18

ow holan yth ew terrys fensan **ow bosaf** *marowe* 'my heart is broken; I would that I were dead' CW 1263-64

So pew a leverough why **y bosama** 'But who do you say that I am?' TH 43a.

5.3.2 2nd person: *bota, bosta*

Me a wothya, parda! the **vota** *ow recordya ow bosa den eredie* 'I knew by God, that you were making known that I was a man indeed' BK 351-53

A te dore, remember y **bosta**, *dore, dore* 'A, you clay, remember that you are clay, clay!' TH 7a

rag y **bosta** *melagas hag in golan re othys der reson thys me a breif* 'that you are accursed and over proud in your heart I will prove by reason to you' CW 305-07

rag ty ny vethys dowtyes drefan y **bosta** *mar deke* 'for you will not be feared because you are so beautiful' CW 523-24

y **bosta** *arluth heb pare in pub place re bo gwerthys* 'that you are a peerless lord may you be revered everywhere' CW 1415-17

me ny allaf convethas y **bosta** *ge ow hendas* 'I cannot understand that you are my grandfather' CW 1609-10

a soweth gwelas an pryes genaf y **bosta** *lethys* 'alas to see the time that you have been killed by me!' CW 1648-49.

5.3.3 3rd person masculine: *bosa*

ha mar te ha gull an dra a ra an perill skynnya anotha wosa y **bosa** *gwarnys y fowt ew the vrassa* 'and if he happen to do the thing from which the danger will come after he has been warned, his sin is the greater' TH 4

§5.3.4   COLLOQUIAL DOESN'T MEAN CORRUPT

*kepar dell vsans y ow cowse, ha penagull a ve diskys then bobyll contrari the henna y **bosa** fals* 'as they speak and whatever was taught to the people contrary thereto is false' TH 19a

*kynth usy pub den ow contya y honyn y **bosa** in charite* 'although everyman considers himself to be in charity' TH 23

*eff a ra supposia y **bosa** saw re bos ragtha* 'he will suppose that it is a too heavy burden for him' TH 24

*An dra ma, tus vas, why a yll inta vnderstondia y **bosa** lell* 'This matter, good people, you will understand to be true' TH 36

*whath dre reson y **bosa** gwrys dre an blonogeth a thu, yth o cryff ha fyrme* 'yet because he was made by the will of God, he was strong and firm' TH 50a

*Praga na russyn ny kyns y ymbrasia ha ry grace the thu ragtha rag y **bosa** an moyha precius Jewall* 'Why did we not rather embrace it and give thanks to God for it for its being the most precious jewel?' TH 54a

*Adam ew gylwys dore dre reson y **bosa** gwrys a dore* 'Adam is called clay because he was made of clay' TH 57a

*yth falsa orth y favoure y **bosa** neb bucka noos* 'he would seem from his appearance to be some bugbear' CW 1588.

5.3.4 3rd person feminine: *bossy*

*han kythsame egglos ma dre reson y **bossy** sanctifies ha benegys…* 'and this same Church because she was sanctified and blessed…' TH 31

5.3.5 1st person plural: *bosen*

*Oll an re ma sure gans mere moy a theth warnan ny dre reson y **bosen** gyllys in mes thean chy a thu* 'All these things indeed with many more have come upon us because we have gone out from the house of God' TH 40a

5.3.6 2nd person plural: *bosowgh*

*Rag henna ow cothmans dre reson y **bosow** gwarnys therag dorne bethow ware* 'Therefore, my friends, since you have been warned beforehand, beware' TH 18

5.3.7 3rd person plural *bosans*

*dre reson y **bosans** y ow pretendya an gyrryow a thu* 'because they claim to have the words of God' TH 19a.

*yma ow settya in mes very notably an primasie han supremite an epscop a Rome y **bosans** an successors, henn ew an sewysy a pedyr* 'he sets out very notabley the primacy and the supremacy of the bishop of Rome, that they are the successors, that is, the followers, of Peter' TH 49

These forms, *bosa, bosaf, bosama*, etc. are well established in historical Cornish. Again one can only ask, why do Nance and his followers ignore them completely?

5.4 THE PLUPERFECT/CONDITIONAL

The pluperfect tense as used today often with the perfective particle *re* is unknown in Middle Cornish outside *Pascon agan Arluth*, for example in:

*gans crist na **vye** tregis* 'that he had not dwelt with Christ' PA 85d
*Then tyller crist re **dothye*** 'Christ had come to the place' PA 33a
*lemen an tol re **wrussens*** 'except the hole which they had made' PA 180d.

After the date of *Pascon agan Arluth* the sense of the pluperfect is rendered by the simple past; a usage which should be the case in the revived language. So, for example, for 'the food had all been eaten before I arrived' would be rendered *Oll an boos o debrys kyns ès me dhe dhos*.

It is interesting in this context to note that Caradar (A. S. D. Smith) writes:

> The same forms do duty for both Pluperfect 'had' and Conditional 'would (have)': this being the meaning when connected with an if-clause (120). The Pluperfect is often preceded by *re*: the Conditional never (1972: 53).

When Caradar says "often preceded by *re*" he is referring exclusively to the examples in *Pascon agan Arluth*, since there are no instances of the pluperfect tense as a pluperfect outside that text. Moreover Caradar also refers to the imperfect with pluperfect sense in two of the examples (8 and 10) cited by him in paragraph 121 on the same page.

Edwin Norris, in his "Sketch of Cornish Grammar" as an appendix for his edition of the three plays of the Ordinalia (1859) was already aware from his reading of the them that the historic pluperfect was not used as a pluperfect. He writes, "In Cornish as far as I have observed, it is used as a conditional only, and it is frequently confounded with the second tense [i.e. the imperfect]" (Norris 1959 ii, 261.

It must be admitted that by seeking to teach students to use the pluperfect as a pluperfect, Caradar was advocating a usage which was already obsolete by the time of the Ordinalia, i.e. the early fifteenth century. Yet as far as most verbs were concerned the pluperfect itself as a conditional was already obsolescent, for it was being replaced by the conditional (originally, pluperfect) of auxiliary verbs *gwil* and *mydnes* followed by the verbal noun of the main verb. Indeed an examination of the texts to find examples of the conditional of full verbs, rather than periphrastic phrases, yielded only 29 examples; of those five were from *Pascon agan Arluth*, and only one from *Beunans Meriasek*. The remaining 23 instances were of the conditional of *cara* 'to love', which in itself was widely used as an auxiliary.

5.5 THE IMPERFECT OF GODHVOS 'TO KNOW'

In the light of what has been said above (3.18) about the loss of medial -*dh*- a colloquial form of *godhvos* 'to know' should be allowed alongside the more literary forms. As an examples let us first use the verb *godhvos* 'to know', giving the forms for all the persons in the negative imperfect, first the standard form, followed by the colloquial form and then the English meaning:

na wo'yen vy	ny wodhyen vy	'I didn't know'
na wo'yes ta	ny wodhyes ta	'you didn't know'
na wo'ya ev	ny wodhya ev	'he didn't know'
na wo'ya hy	ny wodhya hy	'she didn't know'
na wo'yen ny	ny wodhyen ny	we didn't know'
na wo'yewgh why	ny wodhyewgh why	'you *pl*. didn't know'
na wo'yenj y	ny wodhyens y	'they didn't know'.

Note also in the colloquial form above the ending -*ens* appears as -*enj*.

So, translating the English—'I didn't know that', we would have in a modern standardized form *ny wodhyen vy hedna*, and in conversation, *na wo'yen vy hedna*.

Similarly for the English 'Didn't you know he was sick?' in a standardized form we would write *A ny wodhyes ta y vos clâv?* but in conversation and following historical and natural development, *Ny wo'yes ta dell o va clâv*. In the second version the interrogative particle *a* is lost, as is the medial *dh* in the verb. Furthermore the *dell* construction is used to render indirect statement. This latter has been discussed at 5.2–5.2.2 above.

6
PREPOSITIONS

6.1 A PERSONAL PRONOUN IGNORED BY NANCE

Metanalysis, or the wrong division of words, occurs in many languages. In English this has happened for example, with *an nader* > *an adder*, *an ewt* > *a newt*, *a napron* > *an apron* and *a numpire* > *an umpire*. In all these items when preceded by the indefinite article *an* were thought by speakers to begin with a vowel and that the indefinite article was *an* rather than *a*.

Breton is a sister language to Cornish. Some years ago the author received a New Year's card from a fisherman friend who was a Breton speaker, but who could not really write the language. He wrote in his card that the fishing had not been good because of the weather, *A namser a zo fall*, which should have read *An amser a zo fall* 'The weather is bad'. Such false division is frequently encountered in the Cornish texts. An early example can be seen in *Pascon agan Arluth*: *nyn gew ow faynys beghan* 'my torments are not small' PA 166b. Interestingly there are *three* things to note in this one short line:

1. The false division *nyng ew* for *nyng ew*.
2. *g* [dʒ] in *nyng* rather than *s* [z] in *nyns*.
3. One of the only two examples of ⟨gh⟩ in the word for small, *beghan* (Nance's *byghan*).

There is one example of false division which gives rise to a new personal pronoun. This is constantly condemned by some revivalist as badly corrupted and thus to be ignored. Yet the new pronoun was in constant use in the latter part of the seventeenth century. It is variously spelt *angy*, *angye*, *an gye*, *anjy*, *an güe* and *an gee* and was the customary third person plural personal pronoun before a verb, e.g. *angye a gothas* 'they fell' (*y a godhas* in standardized Cornish). It also functioned as the 3rd person plural ending of verbs, e.g. *rag tho an güe* 'for they were' (standard Cornish *rag yth ens y*), *pereg angye* 'when they did' (standard Cornish *pan wrussons y*). On occasion it

71

§6.2   COLLOQUIAL DOESN'T MEAN CORRUPT

also functioned as a post-posited possessive adjective: *ha lagagow an gie* 'and their eyes'. This last usage has probably come about by using *angy* as an emphatic pronoun after the noun on the one hand and suppressing the usual *aga, ga* 'their' before it: **ga lagagow angy* > *lagagow angy*. This construction with possessive *angy*, however, is attested with the third plural only. The second person plural in the later language retains the traditional form, e.g. *agoz lagagow* 'your eyes'

It is unlikely incidentally to have anything to do with expressions like 'eyes of them' in Cornu-English, which would have had to derive from a Cornish phrase like **ha lagagow anongy (*standard Cornish *ha lagajow anedha* or *ha lagajow anodhanjy*), constructions for which there is no evidence at all.

It is apparent how the new pronoun *angy* come about. It certainly derived from the common ending of the third person plural followed by the emphatic third person plural pronoun *-y*. For example, the earlier Cornish ...*dell leverons y* 'as they say' would already in the Middle Cornish period have had a variant in [ondʒ], written ⟨ong⟩. This form *dell leveronj* would have had the main stress on the second syllable of *leveronj*. The unstressed *-onjy*, where unstressed *o* was pronounced as the neutral vowel schwa [ə] was then falsely divided to give a wholly new personal pronoun *angy, anjy*, with the stress on the second syllable.

There is no example of this new personal pronoun until after William Jordan's *Creation of the World* (1611); and there are no instances in the *Creation* itself. There does seem, however, to be one example of the beginnings of the development. In Tregear's Homilies (1555-58) we read: *gesow ny the aswon agan oberow agan honyn fatell engy vnperfect* 'let us acknowledge our own works that they are imperfect' TH: 9a. The clause *fatell engy* shows that already at this period the new pronoun was developing. Notice also the sentence from Sacrament an Alter: *Ima lowarth onyn o bostia fatla vgy faith an tasow coth a vam egglys in an sy* 'Many is the one who boasts that the faith of the ancient father of mother Church is in them' SA 59a. It is quite likely that the scribe who wrote that sentence pronounced *in an sy* with [dʒ] rather than [z]. In which case *in an sy* is an early instance of *in anjy* 'in them'.

The use of *angy* is again a natural development in Cornish. It was rejected by Nance and remains taboo to the advocates of the standardized language, who condemn it as "corrupt" and thus forbidden. Given that *angy* is a natural analogical development, it should no more be condemned than the use of *adder* (earlier *nader*) or *newt* (earlier *ewt*) in Modern English.

6.2 *ANJY* 'THEY' IN LATER TEXTS

Here are some instances of this analogical personal pronoun from the later texts:

*Ha **an chei** woraz an naw penz en dezan* 'And they put the nine pounds in the cake' BF: 16 (NBoson)

*Ha Jooan, a meth **an chei*** 'Ho, John, they said' BF: 16 (NBoson)

mesk angy wonen eu gwenhez ha deskez drez ul an re 'rol 'among them one is skilled and learned beyond all the other' BF: 27 (NBoson)

*dreffen en tacklow broaz ma **angy** mennow hetha go honnen; bus en tacklow minnis, ema **angye** suyah hâz go honnen* 'because in great things they will stretch themselves, but in small matters, they follow their own nature' ACB: E e 3v

*Dew reffa sowia an Egles ni ha an prounterian da eze et **angy*** 'May God save our churches and the clergy in them' LAM: 226 (JTonkin)

*nages prize veeth es moase whath ragt'**angi*** 'but there is not a price set for them yet' LAM: 238 (OPender)

*Pe rêg **an gye** clowaz an matern, y eath caar* 'When they heard the king, they departed' RC 23: 196 (Rowe)

*Ha po tho **an gye** devethez en an choy, y a wellaz an flô yonk* 'And when they had come into the house, they saw the young child' RC 23: 196 (Rowe)

*Ha **an gye** ve gwarnez gen Deew ha an gye a cuskah, ne resa **an gye** doaz ogas tha Herod, ha **an gye** eath carr tha pow go honnen vor arall* 'And they were warned by God when they were sleeping, that they should not approach Herod, and they departed to their own country another way' RC 23: 197 (Rowe).

The above list is by no means exhaustive.

6.3 SIMPLIFICATION OF PREPOSITIONAL PRONOUNS

The earlier forms of the prepositional pronouns were simplified during the history of Cornish. A number of such pronouns are found with the following prepositions: *dhe* 'to, for', *gans* 'with', *er* 'by', *war* 'on', *a* 'of', *dhyworth* 'from', and *rag* 'for'. The simplification occurred in different ways. Most frequently the personal pronoun or a form of it was simply appended to the preposition itself. Although the classical first person and second person forms of *the* (Modern *dhe*), *thym* 'to me' and *thys* 'to thee' are common throughout the Middle Cornish period, the analytical form *tha ve*, *3a ve* 'to me' and *tha gye* 'to thee' are both found in the *Creation of the World*. The *gee* 'to you' is attested in *Sacrament an Alter*. The *ny* 'to us' spelt *theny* is well attested; and *the why* has been common since the time of *Pascon agan Arluth*. In *thym* 'to me', *thys* 'to you' (singular) and *thywgh*, *thewgh* 'to you' (plural) the preposition and the pronoun form one single unit. They are therefore synthetic forms. With forms like *tha ve* 'to me', *tha gye* 'to you' (singular) and *the why* 'to you' (plural) the pronoun appears to have been added to the simple preposition. Such

§6.4   COLLOQUIAL DOESN'T MEAN CORRUPT

forms are described as analytic. In the Cornish prepositional pronouns the shift from synthetic to analytical started early with *thywgh why* becoming *the why* already in *Pascon agan Arluth*. Analytical form, however, are a feature of the later stages of the language.

The third plural form *thethe, thetha* 'to them' has not been replaced by any analytical form. Rather it has been reshaped with the third person plural ending taken from verbs. This gives *thethans* 'to them', and by analogy with the third person singular masculine, *thothans* 'to them'. Third person plural prepositional pronouns like *thethans* 'to them', *gansans* 'with them', *ragthans* 'for them', etc. are found in the later Middle Cornish texts.

Both analogical forms like *thothans* 'to them' and analytical ones like *tha ve* 'to me' are the predominant ones at least from the early seventeenth century onwards. They also provide easy and convenient forms for colloquial use in the revived language.

6.4 PREPOSITIONAL PRONOUNS WITH *THE* 'TO'
Notice that in the following list word division is editorial.

6.4.1 *The vy* 'to me'
dewgh arag omma ʒa vee 'come forward here to me' CW 62
golsowowh tha ve lemyn 'listen to me now' CW 115
creys ʒa ve 'believe me' CW 1615
ha tha ve eve a ornas 'and to me he commanded' CW 1822.

6.4.2 *The gy* 'to thee'
me a laver the gee 'I tell you' SA 62
molath then horsen kam ha tha ge inweth gansa 'curse to the crooked swine and to you also with him' CW 805
a wrug [dew] cowsall tha gye 'did God speak to you?' CW 2349.

6.4.3 *The ny* 'to us, for us'
hef asas vmma e kig the ny 'and he left his flesh for us here' SA 60
blonogath da a thew disquethis the ny 'the good will of God shown to us' SA 60
tha gawas the ny susten 'to get food for us' CW 1081
pew athe wrug gea progowther tha thesky omma the ny 'who made you a preacher to teach us here' CW 2346-47
mynstrels growgh the ny peba 'minstrels, pipe for us' CW 2546.

6.4.4 *The why* 'to you' (plural)
ow thas rom growntyas ʒe wy 'my Father has granted me to you' PA 75c

PREPOSITIONS §6.4.4

ow thus ʒe wy nym delyrfsens yndelma 'my men would not have delivered me thus to you' PA 102bc

fest yn creff me re beghas ihesus ʒe wy ow querʒe 'very greatly have I sinned betraying Jesus to you' PA 104b

me ny wraff pur wyr kentrow ʒe wy vyth 'I will not make any nails for you' PA 155a

kentrow ʒe wy why ny fyll 'nails shall not be lacking to you' PA 158

*Praga a rug du ry **the why** commandment* 'why did God give you a commandment?' TH 3a

*yth ew declariis **the why** pan a dra ew lell charite* 'it has been declared to you what true charity is' TH 25a

*me a alsa eysy y prevy ha largy lowre y thysquethas **the why*** 'I could easily prove and widely enough demonstrate it to you' TH 34a-35

*me a rug y theclaria **the why*** 'I declared to you' TH 35a

*hag eff a re **the why** conforter arell* 'and he will give you another Comforter' TH 36

*hag eff a vith res **the why*** 'and it will be given to you' TH 39a

*Verily, me a levar **the why*** 'Verily, I say unto you' TH 41a

*Ny goyth **the why**, arluth ker an blam warnaf e settya* 'It behoves you not, dear lord, to put the blame on me' BK 467-68

*Me a lever **the why** dowr* 'I will tell you exactly' BK 496

*Nawothow ema gena' na pleg **the why*** 'I have news that will not please you' BK 934-35

*Arluth, **the why** lowena* 'Lord, joy to you' BK 1105

*Bythquath ny ve **the why** parow* 'Never has there been equal to you' BK 1256-57

***The why** me a worhemmyn* 'To you I command' BK 1277

*Cador, lowena **the why*** 'Cador, joy to you' BK 1371

*Lowena **the why**, Augel* 'Joy to you, Augel' BK 1383

*gras e wothvean **the why*** 'I should aknowledge thanks to you' BK 1593

*rag henna e tuth **the why*** 'therefore have I come to you' BK 1597

*Par **the why** suer ny gerth war leer* 'An equal to you indeed does not walk upon the ground' BK 1695-96

*wylcom o'm tyr i wer onowr **the why** pub wyer* 'welcome to my country to great honour for you always' BK 1948-49

*An uhelha Tas roy **the why** gul da!* 'May the highest Father grant to you to do good!' BK 2477-78

*Me a veth **the why** e gows* 'I will dare to speak to you of it' BK 2560, BK 2568

*Lowena **the why** ha ras* 'Joy to you and grace' BK 2562

*Hail **the why** ha lowena!* 'Hail to you and joy!' BK 2600,

§6.4.5   COLLOQUIAL DOESN'T MEAN CORRUPT

meer ew ow cher **the why** *heb mar* 'great is my affection for you indeed' BK 2923-24

ny a ra **the why** *duur-ros* 'we will make rose-water for you' BK 2991

Lowena **the why** *pub prys* 'Joy to you always' BK 3065;

hag inweth **the why** *cheften* 'and chieftain to you also' CW 117

mear a rase **the why** *sera* 'much thanks to you, sir' CW 702

me a vyn **the why** *poyntya service* 'I will appoint a service to you' CW 1062-03

adam pandra whear **the why** 'Adam, what is the matter with you?' CW 1222,

hag y teaf **the why** *arta* 'and I shall come to you again' CW 1760,

devethis yth of omma gans adam ow thase **the why** 'I have come here to you at my father's request' CW 1780-81

chardges yth of in della [gans] ow thas omma **the why** 'I was ordered thus by my father to you here' CW 1788-89,

mear a ras **the why** *eall due* 'great thanks to you, angel of God' CW 1871

Lowena **the why** *ow thas* 'Joy to you, my father' CW 1880

a das kere mere rase **the why** 'O dear father, great thanks to you' CW 1953

benaw ha gorawe omma genaf **the why** *yma dreys* 'male and female I have brought here to you' CW 2416-17,

nyng es tra in bys ma gwryes mes **the why** *a wra service* 'there is nothing created in this world but does you servive' CW 2515-16

Dew re thenenna **the why** *fare e ta* 'God send you to fare well' Borde.

6.4.5 *Thethans, thothans* 'to them'

thethans *y re bo oll honor ha glory bys vyckan* 'to them be all honour and glory for ever' TH 16

eff a rug oll an da a ylly **thethans** *y ha ragthans y* 'he did all the good he could to them and for them' TH 23

eff a ve promysiis **thethans** *y* 'he was promised to them' TH 36a,

Jhesus a leverys **thethans** *y* 'Jesus said to them' TH 43a

hag eff the cowse in generally **thethans** *y oll therag dorne* 'and when he was talking generally to them all beforehand' TH 44a

indella Dew a ros **thothans** *an vse age corfow* 'thus God gave them the use of their bodies' TH 55 *footnote*

whath eth ew gwrys satisfaction **thethans** 'yet it is made satisfaction for them' SA 64

nyng ew **thethans** *Corf Dew* 'they have not the body of God' SA 65a

ro **thothans** *aga henwyn* 'give them their names' CW 400

ha deaw gweth **dothans** *gwra doen* 'and carry to them two garments' CW 967

parys yw genaf pub tra tha vose **thothans** *alemma* 'I have prepared everything to go hence to them' CW 971-12,
dowte sor dew nyng essa **thothans** 'they did not have the fear of the wrath of God' CW 2429-30.

It will be noted in the above list that *the why*, the second person plural, is by far the commonest of the analytical forms of the prepositional pronouns with *the* 'to'. This is probably because the synthetic forms *thywgh why, thewgh why* were phonetically speaking very close to *the why*; as a result *thewgh why* was re-analyzed by speakers as the simple preposition *the* followed by *why* 'you' (plural). Indeed it is quite likely that the re-analysis of *thewgh why* > *the why* was itself the starting point for the analytic forms of the other persons.

6.5 RECOMMENDED PREPOSITIONAL PRONOUNS
In the light of the above discussion, cited here are the recommended colloquial paradigms of prepositional pronouns for *dhe* 'to', *gans* 'with', *yn* 'in', *dhyworth/dhort* 'from', *orth* 'at', *a* 'from', *wàr* 'upon', *dhyrag* 'before', *ryb* 'beside', and *dre* 'through'. Many, though not all the forms are attested in the later sources. The forms listed below are, of course, intended for colloquial use.

6.5.1 *Dhe* 'to'
dhe vy 'to me'
dhe jy 'to you' (singular)
dhodha, dhe ev 'to him'
dhe hy 'to her'
dhe ny 'to us'
dhe why 'to you' (plural)
dhe anjei, dhodhans 'to them'

6.5.2 *Gans/gen* 'with'
gena vy/genama 'with me'
genes jy 'with you' (singular)
gonsa, gans ev 'with him'
gonsy, gonsy hy 'with her'
gena ny 'with us'
gena why 'with you' (plural)
gansans 'with them'

6.5.3 *In* 'in'
ina vy 'in me'
inas jy 'in you' (singular)
ino, eta 'in him'
inhy, etta hy 'in her'
ina ny 'in us'
ino why 'in you' (plural)
inhans, ettans, et anjy 'in them'

6.5.4 *Dhyworth, dhort* 'from'
dhorta vy, dhortam 'from me'
dhorta jy 'from you' singular'
dhorta, dhorta ev 'from him'
dhorta hy 'from her'
dhorta ny 'from us'
dhorto why 'from you' (plural)
dhortans, dhort anjy 'from them'.

COLLOQUIAL DOESN'T MEAN CORRUPT

6.5.5 *Orth* 'at'
ortha vy, orta vy 'at me'
orthys 'at you' (singular)
orta ev 'at him'
orta hy 'at her'
ortha ny 'at us'
ortha why 'at you' (plural)
ortans, orta anjy 'at them'

6.5.6 *A* 'from, of'
ahana vy 'of me'
ahanasta 'of you' (singular)
anodha 'of him'
anodhy 'of her'
ahana ny 'of us'
ahana why 'of you' (plural)
anodhans, anonj 'of them'

6.5.7 *Wàr* 'upon'
warna vy 'upon me'
warna jy 'upon you' (singular)
warnodha 'upon him'
warnedhy 'upon her'
warna ny 'upon us'
warna why 'upon you' (plural)
war anjy 'upon them'

6.5.8 *Rag* 'for'
raga vy, ragama 'for me'
ragas jy 'for you' (singular)
racta 'for him'
racty 'for her'
raga ny 'for us'
raga why 'for you' (plural)
ragthans, ract anjy 'for them'

6.5.9 *Dhyrag, dyrag* 'before, in front of'
dhyraga vy, dyraga vy 'before me'
dhyragas jy, dyragas jy 'before you' (singular)
dhyracta, dyracta 'before him'
dhyracty, dyracty 'before her'
dhyraga ny, dyraga ny 'before us'
dhyraga why, dyraga why 'before you' (plural)
dhyractans, dyractans, dhyract anjy, dyract anjy 'before them'

6.5.10 *Ryb* 'beside'
ryba vy, rybama 'beside me'
rybas jy 'beside you' (singular)
repto 'beside him'
repty 'beside her'
ryba ny 'beside us'
ryba why 'beside you' (plural)
rept anjy 'beside them'

6.5.11 *Dre* 'through'
dredha vy 'through me'
dredhas jy 'through you' (singular)
dredh'ev 'through him'
dredha hy 'through her'
dredha ny 'through us'
dredha why 'through you' (plural)
dredh anjy 'through them'.

7
PROBLEMS IN THE LEXICON

Nicholas Williams has provided a comprehensive review of questions related to the lexicon of revived Cornish in his book *Geryow Gwir*. I will mention two items only as examples of a particular type of infelicitous usage.

7.1 *ARHANS* 'SILVER' AND *MONA* 'MONEY'
Necessity demands that the vocabulary of Cornish must be expanded from time to time, particularly when no exact equivalent can be found in the texts. Over the years, however, some words have been devised or adapted from original sources and their meaning has been changed. Often now such items have two distinct meanings, one traditional, the other less so. A good example is the word *arhans*. Although speakers of revived Cornish use the word *arhans* to mean 'silver', the only original meaning, they also use it to mean 'money'. In the traditional Cornish texts, however, *arhans* does not mean 'money', which is invariably *mona*. Here are the attestations of these two items:

7.1.1 *Arhans* 'silver'
owr hag **arghans** *gwels ha gweth* 'gold and silver, grass and trees' PA 16b

an **arghans** *a gemeras* 'the silver that he took' PA 103b

fenten bryght avel **arhans** 'a spring as bright as silver' OM 771

my a vyn vos garlont gureys a **arhans** *adro thethe* 'I wish that a garland made of silver be placed round them' OM 2096-97

yma onen theugh parys a **arans** *pur ha fyn gurys* 'one has been made ready for you made of pure and fine silver' OM 2099-100

vn pren gans garlontow a **arhans** *adro thotho* 'a beam with garlands of silver around it' OM 2499-2500

an **arhans** *kettep dyner me a's deghes war an luer* 'the silver, every penny, I will cast upon the floor' PC 1514-15

§7.1.2   **COLLOQUIAL DOESN'T MEAN CORRUPT**

*en **arhans** me a gymer hagh a's guyth kettep dyner* 'I will take the silver and will keep every penny of them' PC 1538-39

*awos cost **arhans** nag our greugh y tenne mes a'n dour* 'despite the cost in silver and gold, do you draw him out of the water' RD 2230-31

*lavar war cota dean brose en **arg[h]anz** hunt tho canz bloath coth lebben* 'a motto on a gentleman's coat of arms in silver over a hundred years old now' BF: 27 (NBoson)

*An pelle **arrance** ma ve resse gen mere hurleyey, creve ha brasse, do Wella Gwavas, an deane gentle* 'This golden ball was given by many hurlers strong and great to William Gwavas the gentleman' BF: 38 (TBoson).

7.1.2 *Mona* 'money'

*trehans dynar a **vone*** 'three hundred pence of money' PA 36a

xxx (leg. *dek warn ugens*) *a **vone** yn vn payment y wrens ry* 'that they would give thirty pieces of money in one payment' PA 39d

*ow box mennaf the terry a dal mur a **vone** da* 'I will break my box which is worth much good money' PC 485-86

*dek warn ugens a **mone** me ny vennaf cafus le* 'thirty pieces of money; I won't take less' PC 593-94

*rak henna an guella vs dascor myns **mone** yv pys* 'therefore the best thing is to forfeit as much money as has been paid' PC 1507-08

*otte an **mone** parys thy'so the pe* 'here is the money ready to pay you' PC 1556

*ha me a vyn then benenes ry **mona*** 'and I will give money to the women' BM 1671-72

*due yv an **mona** rum fay* 'upon my faith the money has run out' BM 1873

*yma **mona** gans henna* 'that man has money' BM 1904

*sav dascor ol the **vona*** 'but hand over all your money' BM 1917

*Ith ew scryffys in viii-as chapter in actys an appostolis fatell rug Symon magus offra the ry **mona** the pedyr* 'It is written in the eighth chapter of the Acts of the Apostles that Simon Magus offered to give money to Peter' TH 46a

*Ha an **mona** an dzhei a gavaz* 'And they found the money' BF: 19

*Loan blethan noueth ha bennen joungk: ha **mona** lour gans goz gureg* 'A joyful new year and a young woman: and may your wife have money enough' BF: 45 (JBoson)

*Ni venja pea a **munna** seer ez boaze whelees car thurt an tir* 'We would pay the money certainly that is being sought from far afield' LAM: 226 (JTonkin)

*Dry dre an **mona** ha perna moy* 'Bring home the money and buy more' ACB F fv.

*Pecunia…Money…C[ornish] **Monnah*** AB: 115c.

From these examples it can be seen that *arhans* has the meaning of 'silver', and *mona* has the meaning of 'money' only. Possibly where the confusion had arisen was from two references in *Pascon Agan Arluth*. The first at stanza 39 relates how Judas Iscariot asked the Jews how much would they give hime to betray Christ, and they agreed 'thirty pieces of money'. Then in stanza 103, the text reads *an arghans a gemeras* 'the *silver* that he took'. Nance however translated this as 'the *money* that he took'. It is obvious that the money given was in silver, as shown by these two references, and that Nance knew this, but quite possibly inadvertently translated *ar(g)hans* as 'money'. Thus was the seed sown for *arhans* henceforward to be accepted in the revival as the ordinary word for 'money'.

With so many words relating to finance in today's Cornish vocabulary that are all built on the word *arhans*, it would not be practical in many instances to change them. The word for 'bank' is an exception. Cornish could quite easily use *bank*, plural *bancow*, for 'bank', rather than *arhanty. After all the word *bank* is virtually the same in all European languages. Caradar also used *bank* for 'bank'. When 'money' *per se* is used however, the word should be *mona*; *arhans* should be used only when silver coinage is involved. *Arhans* ought otherwise be retained for the metal.

7.2 SPURIOUS COINAGE

Tavern is the only word for 'tavern, public house' found in the Cornish text: *in* **tavern** *sur ov eva ymons pur ruth age myn* 'indeed they are drinking in the pub and their mouths are very red [with wine]' BM 3308-09. Lhuyd also cites **tavargn** 'caupona' [tavern, inn] AB: 47a and **tshy tavarn** 'taberna' [tavern, inn] AB: 160b. Pryce gives **TAVARGN**, *tshyi tavargn*, 'a tavern, an alehouse, a victualling-house' ACB Y4 verso.

The word now universally used for 'pub' these days, however, is *dewotty, *dywotty. This word is wholly unattested, having been invented by Nance for his 1938 dictionary on the basis of the obsolete Welsh word *dioty* 'alehouse, public house'. It is noteworthy that in his earlier dictionary of 1934 for 'ale-house' Nance cites *chy-tavern* from Lhuyd, and for 'pub' he uses *tavern*; his own newly created *dewotty* is absent. There seems to be no justification for the use the invented word *dewotty when *tavern* is actually attested.

Much of the problem is of course, that many users of Cornish do not like borrowings from English. The question remains, however, if words borrowed from English are attested, when modern coinages are not, what conceivable reason is there to prefer the unattested coinage to the attested borrowing? Again we seem to be dealing with the whole question of a pure, ideal language, untainted by admixture with English.

§7.3 COLLOQUIAL DOESN'T MEAN CORRUPT

If a lexical item is poorly attested and if its provenance is difficult to ascertain, then there can be little objection to using a modern coinage, or preferably a borrowed word instead. If on the other hand a newly-coined word is of doubtful parentage, and a well-attested borrowing is available, the borrowed item should be preferred—even though some purists may object.

7.3 QUESTIONS AND ANSWERS

Many enthusiastic beginners in their attempts at spoken Cornish are very concerned about "getting things right", but such enthusiasm is often excessive and unwarranted. Of course, presenting an official paper to an attentive audience is a different thing from informal conversation; but speech is mostly in conversation, and there adhering to strict rules can make conversation boring and uninteresting. Many people try too hard to be unnecessarily precise in the hope that ten unnecessary words are going somehow to make their Cornish sound imposing and of high quality. Some examples will suffice.

Students are taught in classes, that when answering a question, the verb of the question, must appear in the appropriate form in the answer. For example, the student is told that in answering the question, *Esos ta ow mos dhe Drûrû avorow?*, the affirmative answer should at least be, *Esof.* Moreover, if the speaker wishes, he may repeat much of the remainder of the question, so that the answer becomes, *Esof, yth esof vy ow mos.* If the answer is negative, the speaker should at least say, *Nag esof, nyns esof vy ow mos.* Grammatically of course this is all correct, but one asks oneself in what sort of conversation would that be heard? The student is told that a question of this kind should never be answered with a straight, *Eâ* or *Nâ*. But we are talking about contemporary spoken Cornish. To repeat everything "by the book" is archaic and far too rigid. It cannot be repeated too often—the spoken language should be vibrant and expressive, rather than follow strict grammatical rules—which if broken condemn the speaker to everlasting hell fire! Where even in "perfect" English would you hear the following?

Do you go to Truro very often?
I do or, *I do not.*

The answer is much more likely be, *Yes* with probably a little addition such as *if I can* or something similar to be polite, or *No, I can't.* Similarly, in a conversation in Cornish, if the above question were posed, then the answer could follow a number of different routes, e.g.

PROBLEMS IN THE LEXICON §7.3

Esos ta ow mos dhe Drûrû avorow?
Eâ, dell brederaf, or, *Martesen, mar pÿdh termyn,* or, *Nâ, my yw re sqwith.*

This is a conversation not a formal oral examination. How boring the conversation becomes when all the rules are followed to the letter as follows:

Esos ta ow mos dhe Drûrû avorow?
Esof, yth esof vy ow mos, dell brederaf i'n eur-ma, or, *Esof, mar pÿdh termyn dhybm mos dy,* or, *Nag esof, nyns esof vy ow mos. Re sqwith ov i'n eur-ma.*

The author can well remember a get-together many years ago in which a particular speaker was always very enthusiastic about "getting everything right", and in so doing, often got himself tied up in so many knots— grammatically speaking—that the resultant answer would turn out inordinately long and unnecessarily complicated. He was asked a perfectly simple question, something like this:

Pyw o va a leverys hedna?

Instead, however, of his answer being simple and straightforward, such as:

An den i'n gornel-na, or more bluntly, *Ev y'n gornel na,*

he attempted to elucidate everything and the final result was:

An den na ujy owth esedha i'n gader mayth yw desedhys i'n gornel-na.

Of course, this problem is not specific to Cornish. Every living language has its more colloquial register where strict grammar is sometimes disregarded entirely. It is only in a dead language, Latin for example, where the strict rules of sentence structure are followed meticulously. This is certainly not true for Cornish. The words of William Scawen, writing when the language was still the vernacular, are worth quoting here, for he says that Cornish was "….lively and manly spoken…"

We have already discussed the reduction of-*rdh*-to -*rr*. We would would translate 'Do you walk everyday for your health?' into literary Cornish as *A wrewgh why kerdhes pùb dëdh rag agas yêhes?* Colloquially, however, it would be *Wrew why kerres pùb dedh ra'gas yêhes?*

It is also interesting to note here that if the singular form of 'you' were used in this sentence, then this in standardized Cornish is already acceptable as *wreta* where the medial *-dh-* has been assimilated to the following *t*. We would not say **a wredh ta*?

7.4 THE ABSURDITY OF INFLECTIONAL ARCHAISM WITH MODERN NEOLOGISMS

Another reason for these obsolescent and/or obsolete forms to be avoided in modern Cornish is that modern conversation requires modern terminology. This sits badly with archaizing grammar. How can grammatical forms and constructions, which were already obsolescent by the fifteenth century be wedded to lexical items coined in the first half of the twentieth century, to say nothing of terms coined in this century?

We don't hear contemporary English conversations in Shakespearean or Chaucerian English alongside modern neologisms. For example, how ridiculous the following would sound:

> Bill: *Lat us hange oute thys weekende and thou shalt haven all the magique thou needst. Yn sooth, rokke on!*
> John: *Hast thou seen my cell phone? Ich hadde yt right here.*
> Bill: *What sorte ys yt?*
> John: *Yt ys yclept Samsung.—Ah, yt ys okaye, here yt is.*
> Bill: *Woldest thou consider retweetinge thys upon thy twitter site?*
> John *Verily I shal, but what is yt?*
> Bill: *Yt cometh from Reg and quoth he, 'One millioun retweetes and Kynge Arthur shal retourne to the worlde'.*

Amusing perhaps, but ridiculous and would *never* be said in a serious manner. The same incongruous mixture of linguistic archaism and modern terminology is to a certain extent what is found in current Cornish usage— a mixture of all eras.

Here is a Cornish example of a similar situation which could happen everyday:

> "Hèm yw tyller teg," yn medh ev, "Pÿth yw y hanow?"
> "Y'n gylwyr Trevarghek," y teuth an gorthyp, "hag y hyllyr gweles an airborth i'n pellder."
> "Pur vrâs yw an airborth, a nynj yw? Pygebmys jynys ebron a yll ev sensy?"
> "Adro dhe gans, dell brederaf."
> "Res yw dhybm textya dhe'm broder ha leverel dhodho in y gever."
> "Te a yll assaya, mès nynj eus sînel obma rag clapgûth."

That dialogue is written largely in what is termed Middle Cornish. It contains two examples of a somewhat archaic item of accidence *(y'n gylwyr* and *y hyllyr)*. It also contains one spelling and therefore pronunciation wholly absent from any of the Cornish texts, namely *Trevarghek*. On the other hand it uses modern neologisms, eg. *clapgûth* and *textya*. This hotchpotch of medieval language and spelling (some of it archaic even in the Middle Ages) is bizarre. The author of such a passage in English would be laughed out of court.

7.5 THE QUESTION OF NEW WORDS

Incidentally the question of new coinages necessary for discussing contemporary matters is worth examing. In the Cornish revival generally there is still a certain resistance to the coining of new words. The fact is, however, that a conversation in Cornish about modern topics and modern notions is impossible, if the speaker confines himself or herself exclusively to items attested in the texts and in traditional word-lists, i.e. Lhuyd, Pryce, Borlase, etc. Yet one often hears people saying: "You can't say that, they didn't have a word for that when Cornish was in use." Fortunately this attitude is gradually disappearing, but some people have an almost irrational opposition to modern coinages. Even if one were to use only those items of the Cornish lexicon that were found in Late Cornish texts from, say, the early eighteenth century, the vocabulary would already be 300 years out-of-date. To countenance only the lexicon of the historic Middle Cornish texts—as has been often recommended—as a basis for modern speech, would be to confine oneself to a vocabulary at least 500 years out-of-date!

The author can remember being told that a very much respected and loyal member of the language revival—admittedly some 30 or so years ago—who asserted without a hint of irony, that "there was no need to invent new words, as all the words you needed could be found in the texts". The author has so far failed to find so many of the words necessary for a contemporary conversation in these same historical texts.

Admittedly, a certain amount of common sense has to prevail in the coining of the necessary new words in an ever-expanding modern vocabulary, and we should not slavishly accept a word directly from another language. This is possible in English, and indeed modern English is very different from Old English (Anglo Saxon) and Middle English, owing to a great extent to the influence of French after the Norman Conquest in the eleventh century. English continues to absorb lexical items from other languages.

§7.5 COLLOQUIAL DOESN'T MEAN CORRUPT

Such wholesale borrowing is probably not the best way forward for Cornish, as a huge importation of foreign words would ensure that the language would follow the same path as English and become unrecognizable as a distinct language. Cornish already contains a relatively large number of English and French words, which were adopted in the Middle Ages. This does not mean that the language must not change and evolve—it has to for it to be a modern, vibrant, usable language. No change means eventual extinction. As someone once said: "You can either sit still and fight change, and you will fail, or you can embrace it and move on."

So what is the recommendation for neologisms? The current process reminds the author of the old comment about a camel, and how it was invented by a committee. New words should come into the vocabulary naturally and by those who are continually using and speaking it. The committee process of working out new words so that they can be put into a dictionary inevitably leads to a committee-style invention. The words may have been carefully devised, even on ideological principles, but often, nonetheless, they *sound* invented. In modern languages, everyday and non-technical new words are not coined by a board or committee, they are derived naturally by the speakers, and if they become universally accepted, then they find their way into a dictionary. Most technical, scientific and medical words are derived from the classical languages, Greek and Latin, and more often than not they find their way into other languages comparatively unchanged.

Frequently the question is heard: "What is the word for x?" Almost as frequently the reply comes, "The panel have decided on y and that will be in the dictionary that is in preparation." This is without doubt a passport for an officially approved and fabricated vocabulary.

Shakespeare himself is reputed to have invented or coined over sixteen thousand words, many of which are in current use today, for example, *countless*, *critical*, *excellent*, *lonely*, *majestic*, and *obscene*. Obviously in order to express himself clearly, he found the need to introduce a large number of new words. If *he* needed to do that in *his* time, where change was generally very slow, how much more necessary it is to create neologisms in today's much faster expanding technological world, and this is particularly true for Cornish

8
COUNTING IN CORNISH

A revision of the Cornish system of numerals is imperative if the language is to be suitable for present-day need. It might be claimed that to revise the system of numbers is to violate the essential argument of this work, namely, that the revived language should base itself entirely on natural developments in the language. A wholesale recasting of the numerals is the very opposite of such a position. This argument is based on a misunderstanding, as will become clear.

There are many reasons to support the shift of the Cornish numeral system from one based on twenties to a simpler one based on tens. It is essential, if the language is to be used a workable medium for daily use, that the numbers be reworked. This is particularly true for the use of numerals in speech, rather than in written form.

One obvious factor behind such a revision is that nowadays many numbers are of a magnitude unheard of in the Middle Ages. In that period when Cornish was the vernacular in most of Cornwall, large numbers would have been rare, especially among everyday working people, fishermen, tinners, farmers and their wives. As a good starting point let us look at wages. In Cornwall today a tradesman will earn, say £12.50 an hour, which for a day of eight hours is £100. For a five-day week this amounts to £500 and thus to £26,000 per annum. Compare this with the earnings of an average skilled tradesman of 1560. His daily wage would have been 8½d a day (3½p in modern decimal currency) and about 4 shillings and threepence (21p) a week. That is to say £11.1s (£11.05) per annum.

The numbers quoted above for modern wages are simple enough, but if we put them exactly as the figures were given for the sixteenth-century century tradesman, then the earnings of today's tradesman would look approximately as follows: hourly rate: £12.34, which gives £493.60 a week and £25,667.20 per annum. At this point things become more difficult. It would have been easy enough for a tradesman of *c.* 1560 to say *ow gober vy i'n vledhen yw udnek puns hag udn sols* 'my annual wages are eleven pounds and one shilling'. His modern counterpart, however, would have to say: *Ow gober vy i'n vledhen yw pymp mil warn ugans, whegh cans, seyth ha try ugans puns hag ugans dynar,* literally 'My annual earnings are five thousand upon twenty, six hundred, seven and three score pounds and twenty pence'. This is not only long-winded, it is confusing as well. How many large numbers would the average person have used *c.* 1560? Not many, certainly, as there was very little need of them. Wages could be reckoned in small numbers, as is shown above; moreover the cost of food and everyday items was usually no more than a few pence or shillings—anything costing a pound for the average Cornishman or Cornishwoman in the second half of the sixteenth century would have been a great rarity. An examination of wills and legacies, even of the richer tradesmen, indicates that the value of their possessions amounted to a few shillings at most. The bulk of legacies were made in kind, in pieces of furniture, pottery or cutlery, for instance, or in the case of farmers, an animal or two. Nowadays, if we exclude the animals, most of such sixteenth-century legacies would be discarded, unless they had value as heirlooms. In all probability the largest number that sixteenth-century Cornishmen and Cornishwomen would have needed to discuss, would have been people's ages. Probably the largest number these people would have had to deal with would have been people's ages, and here 80 or 90 would have been the maximum. Would such people need to use thousands? Possibly they might on occasion have needed to state a particular date *Anno Domini*. This seems to have been rare, since documents from this period often gave the date, for example, as the '*n*th' year of the monarch's reign—and that for the ordinary person on no more than a very few occasions. Indeed the first exact reference to a year is attested the translation of King Charles's letter: *in blethan myll whegh cans dewgans ha try* 'in the year one thousand, six hundred and forty-three'. This is dated *c.* 1707 (Keigwin).

The number 'thousand' was obviously known to them, but it is doubtful whether they would have need to use it. There was nothing which they encountered in their lifetimes which would have required a large figure, especially an exact figure of say, 'one thousand five hundred and forty-three'. If on the rare occasion there was something which they were describing was of a price or number far beyond their usual reckoning, it would have been roundly referred to *'as much as a thousand'* or *'over a thousand'* and on very rare occasions, *'thousands'*. It is unlikely that the ordinary Cornish-speaker would have needed to refer explicitly to specific large numbers.

COUNTING IN CORNISH §8

Numbers as large as a thousand or larger are attested in the Cornish text. The word *mil* 'thousand' occurs several times as do the phrases *dyw vil* 'two thousand' and *teyr mil* 'three thousand'. One also finds *milyow cans* 'a hundred thousand' and *cans mil* 'a hundred thousand;' *deg milblek* 'ten thousand times' is also attested. *Milweyth* 'a thousand times' occurs and *milvil* 'a thousand thousand' is attested three times. *Try mylyon* 'three million' is attested once. Outside of these few numerical references, there is nowhere found one example of an exact large number, such as '*two thousand three hundred and fourteen*'.

Things are very different today. Large numbers are as common among ordinary people—wages, the price of cars and houses, and other large, and extremely large, figures are in daily use. In English such numbers are manageable. In Cornish, however, even some of the smaller numbers are very complicated, so say nothing of numbers involving thousands or millions. Without doubt there is an urgent need to simplify the way we deal with such numbers in Cornish. Of course, some people when they read what has been written above will protest that there is no need to revise what is working well. Such people will doubtless assert that they can manage perfectly easily. One wonders how many people, when reading a passage in Cornish to themselves and meeting a date or other large number, read it in English?

Here a simple experiment is suggested. Ask someone who claims to be fairly fluent in Cornish to read out aloud to an audience a couple of lengthy paragraphs containing many dates and big numbers. Doubtless that when the reader comes across these numbers, he or she will have to start thinking very hard in an attempt to remain fluent, and will be glad when the last number has been passed. If the reader is offered the same passage—but in English—and is asked to read it out aloud as before, the dates and large numbers will not present him or her with any problem at all. Why should this be? In the first place English numerals are far simpler to use than their Cornish equivalents. Moreover when attempting to use Cornish at *Yeth an Weryn* or a similar event, speakers very frequently use round numbers and approximation in order to avoid the cumbersome Cornish numbers of the vicesimal system. The author has himself actually done such an experiment. When Cornish-speaking subjects were asked to quote the price of a new television set, for example, at £495.99, rather than grapple with *peswar cans, pymthek ha peswar ugans puns, nawnjek ha peswar ugans dynar* invariably said something like *ogas lowr dhe bymp cans puns*.

The author can well remember on one occasion when he had to give a talk at a language "open day"—a talk which involved a considerable number of dates—and as he was delivering his talk, it was clear to see that

§8   COLLOQUIAL DOESN'T MEAN CORRUPT

the audience were struggling to try and understand these dates as the talk was proceeding. They may not have been aware that it showed on their faces, but it was easy to see from his position, with their eyes rapidly "searching" some invisible database and unconsciously trying to work them out.

Another situation where a radical change to the vicesimal system would be most welcome is when one is attempting to write down large figures from dictation. A figure which is heard rather than read is always difficult to write down—for example, at a meeting where finances are being discussed and the treasurer cites the balance for a particular date. When the treasurer says in Cornish *teyr mil, pymp cans, dewdhek ha...* 'three thousand, five hundred and...', the person writing the minutes is unable to write anything after the *cans...* until he or she hears what the score or vicesimal part of the number involves. Probably not important to many people, but of relevance to the problem.

Why then do we struggle with something which is unnecessarily complicated when a much simpler system is available? As stated earlier, where relatively very small numbers are being only occasionally used, as in days gone by, then a more complicated system is not of particular concern. When, however, we find it necessary to start using much longer numbers very frequently, then a simpler and more convenient system has to be sought.

Of course, numbers and meaurement in twenties or scores are by no means unique to Cornish and these were also a feature in English centuries ago. Indeed the author himself remembers when he was a boy helping on a farm the weights of pigs were invariably given in scores of pounds. The more generally accepted and indeed long accepted model in English is to reckon in tens. A similar system has recently proposed for Cornish, which the author whole-heartedly supports it.

Why was the former British currency of pounds, shillings and pence replaced by the simpler decimal coinage system? In the old system one had to add up a list of prices, for example in a shopping-list, for example: 14/6d + 3/8¾d + 9/2½d + 11¼d + 1/8½d etc., possibly with ten or more items. People who remember such a system, will surely agree that the decimal system, when it was introduced, simplified matters greatly.

The same difficulties applied with measurements. If one compares the British imperial system of feet, inches and fractions of an inch to the metric system, one sees at a glance which of the two is the easier. It is very much easier to add the metric lengths 857mm and 1,376mm than their imperial equivalents: 2′ 9¾″ and 4′ 5⅞″. In the same way it is far easier to multiply the metric lengths $5.242m \times 6.671m$ than to multiply the imperial equivalents: 17′ 3⅜″ × 21′ 10⅝″. Even with a calculator the imperial numbers cause problems, because calculators cannot conveniently deal with vulgar fractions.

In the light of the above, it seems curious that there is any debate about the necessity of modernizing the Cornish system of numeration. The old adage "if it was good enough for my father, it is good enough for me" should be dismissed. Let us make the change and without further ado!

Welsh also has a system such as Cornish based on twenties and the Welsh system is even more complicated than Cornish when dealing with numbers in the teens. Although this system is still used by a number of people in Wales, the Welsh are now happily using a system based on ten. One has only to listen to the Archdruid speaking at the Eisteddfod to realize that decimal system of counting in Welsh is now generally accepted.

This simplified system in Cornish should also incorporate, as do the Welsh, a much simpler version for dates, which have always been very cumbersome in spoken and written Cornish. How awkward a number sounds—and often so difficult to understand for the listener—when someone reads for example 'he was born in 1973' in Cornish it appears as *ev a veu genys in mil, naw cans, tredhek ha try ugans*. A decimal system like that used in Welsh would in Cornish simply say: *ev a veu genys in mil, naw seyth try*.

Here then are some examples which exemply the decimal system being recommended. The English is cited first, then the Cornish according to the vicesimal system (CV) and then the recommended decimal form (CD):

75—seventy-five
pymthek ha try ugans CV
seyth deg pymp CD

345—three hunded and forty-three
tryhans try ha dew ugans CV
tryhans peswar deg try CD

4, 791—four thousand, seven hundred and ninety-one
peder mil, seyth cans, unnek ha peswar ugans CV
peder mil, seyth cans, naw deg onen CD

234,557—two hundred and thirty-four thousand, five hundred and fifty seven
dew cans peswardhek warn ugans mil, pymp cans, seytek ha dew ugans CV
dew cans try deg peder mil, pymp cans pymp deg seyth CD

1721—Seventeen twenty-one
Mil, seyth cans, onen warn ugans CV
Mil, seyth dew onen CD

1957—Nineteen fifty-seven
Mil, naw cans, seytek ha dew ugans CV
Mil, naw pymp seyth CD.

It has to be noted of course that although proposals of any change to Cornish should be submitted for comment—and approval, no board, committee or council can dictate what shall or shall not be used. The development of a language is shaped solely by its speakers.

9
WELLA ROWE

9.1 THE CORNISH OF WELLA ROWE

One may legitimately ask: What in fact *is* this Late Cornish corruption to which we have already referred? Naturally there were changes, but these were natural developments of the language—as there were, and still are, in any language. It is more than likely, particularly from a non-academic point of view, that in the very irregular spelling of these later texts Cornish was in this respect little different from English, since Cornish still lacked any standard orthography. As a result the scribes spelt a word in the way it sounded to them—and this could change in the same sentence, the same word was used in different contexts. This seemed to be particularly the case in Cornish of the later era—and to a certain extent in the Middle Cornish texts. This in the present author's opinion is the reason that the Cornish of the seventeenth century in particular appears to contemporary revivalists to be corrupt, or even incorrect. The most we can say is that it seems very different from what is in use today.

Set out below are two short passages from biblical translations by Wella Rowe, one from Genesis and the other from St Matthew's Gospel. Both are written in a fluent and natural style. Rowe was writing at a time when the orthography of the medieval texts was no longer being taught and to some degree Rowe uses a spelling based on English. It is also apparent, however, that some aspects of the traditional spelling of Cornish survived. Each excerpt is given exactly as Rowe himself wrote; although punctuation, capitalization and word division are editorial. After each excerpt is appended a respelling in the colloquial register of Kernowek Standard. Thereafter the same text is cited in the literary register of Kernowek Standard. It will be seen clearly below how perfectly suited is Rowe's Cornish to be the basis of spoken revived Cornish.

§9.2 COLLOQUIAL DOESN'T MEAN CORRUPT

9.2 ROWE'S CORNISH TRANSLATION OF GENESIS 3:1-14

A. Rowe's Genesis 3:1–5 in its original spelling

1 Lebben an hagar-breeve o mouy foulze vell onen vethell an Bestaz an gweale a reege an Arleth Deew Geele; Ha e a lavarraze tha an Vennen, Eah! Reeg Deew lawle, Che na raze debre a kenevrah gwethan an Looar?

2 Ha an venen a lavarraz tha an hagar-breeve, ni a ell debre a thore oll an gweth an loar.

3 Boz thort an gwethan a ez en crease an Loar, Deew a lavarraz why nara debre anethe na narewa e thotcha, lez why a varaw.

4 Ha an hagar-breeve a lavarraz than Vennen, why nara seere merwall.

5 Rag Deew a ore, a en jorna ah ero debre nothe, nena agoz Lagagow ra bos geres; ha why ra boaze pocara deew a cothaz Da ha Droag

B. Rowe's Genesis 3:1–5 in KS (*colloquial register*)

1 Lebmyn an hager-brÿv o moy fâls 'vell onen vŷth oll a'n bestas a'n gwel a wrug an Arlùth Duw gwil. Ha ev a lavaras dha'n venyn, Eâ! 'Wrug Duw lawl, Che na wras debry a kenyver gwedhen a'n lowarth?

2 Ha an venyn a lavaras dha'n hager-brÿv, Ny a ell debry adhorth oll an gwëdh a'n lowarth.

3 Bùs dhort an gwedhen a eus in cres an lowarth, Duw a lavaras: Why na wra debry anodhy nâ na wrewgh hy thùchya, lès why a verow.

4 Ha an hager-brÿv a lavaras dha'n venyn: Why na wra sur merwel.

5 Rag Duw a or, a udn jorna a wrewgh debry anodhy, i'n eur-na agas lagajow 'wra bos egerys; ha why 'wra bos pecar ha Duw o codhos dâ ha drog.

C. Rowe's Genesis 3:1–5 in KS (*literary register*)

1 Lebmyn an hager-brÿv o moy fâls avell onen vÿth oll a'n bestas a'n gwel a wrug an Arlùth Duw gwil. Hag ev a leverys dhe'n venyn, Eâ! 'Wrug Duw leverel, Te na wras debry a kenyver gwedhen a'n lowarth?

2 Ha'n venyn a leverys dhe'n hager-brÿv, Ny a yll debry adhyworth oll an gwëdh a'n lowarth.

3 Mès dhyworth an gwedhen a eus in cres an lowarth, Duw a leverys: Why ny wrewgh debry anedhy nâ ny wrewgh hy thùchya, lès why a verow.

4 Ha'n hager-brÿv a leverys dhe'n venyn: Why ny wra sur merwel.

5 Rag Duw a wor, an udn jorna a esowgh ow debry anodhy, nena agas lagajow 'wra bos egerys; ha why 'wra bos pecar ha Duw ow codhvos dâ ha drog.

A. Rowe's Genesis 3:6–10 in its original spelling

6 Pereege a Vennin gwellas tro an wethan da rag booze, ha derohi blonk than Lagagow ha gwethan tha voaze desyryes tha gwelle onen feere; Hi a gomeras radn an Haze anethe ha reege debre; ha a rowze radn the e Goore goshe, hag e reege debre.

7 Ha lagagow an gie ve gerres ha an gie oyah teler an gie en noath; ha an gye a wrovas Delkyow Figgez warbarth, ha wraze tho an gye aprodnieo.

8 Ha angye a glowhas leaufe a Arleth Deew a kerras en Looar en yeindre an Deeth, ha Adam ha e wreege a geeth tha govah thort deraage an Arleth Deew amisk an gweeth an Looar.

9 Ha an Arleth Deew agerias tha Adam ha lavarraz thotha peleha estha?

10 Ha e lavarraz, Ve a glowhas tha leave en loohar; ha me a vee owne, rag theren en noath, me geath tha govah.

B. Rowe's Genesis 3:6–10 in KS (*colloquial register*)

6 Pa wrug an venyn gweles dell o an wedhen dâ rag boos, ha dell o hy blonk dhe'n lagajow ha gwedhen dhe vos desîrys dhe wil onen fur, hy a gemeras radn a'n has anodhy ha wrug debry; ha a ros radn dha hy gour gonsy, ha e wrug debry.

7 Ha'ga lagajow y a veu egerys ha anjy a woya dell era anjy yn noth; hag y a wrovas dêlyow fygys warbarth, ha wras dho anjy aprodnyow.

8 Ha anjy a glôwas lev an Arlùth Duw ow kerdhes i'n lowarth in yêynder an dëdh, hag Adam ha'y wreg êth dhe gudha dhorth dyrag an Arlùth Duw in mesk an gwëdh a'n lowarth.

9 Ha'n Arlùth Duw a grias dhe Adam hag a lavaras dhodho: Py le esta?

10 Ha e a lavaras, Ve a glôwas dha lev i'n lowarth; ha ve a veu own, rag th'eren yn noth, me êth dha gudha.

C. Rowe's Genesis 3:6–10 in KS (*literary register*)

6 Pàn wrug an venyn gweles dell o an wedhen dâ rag boos, ha dell o hy blonk dha'n lagajow ha gwedhen dha vos desîrys dhe gwil onen fur, hy a gemeras radn a'n has anodhy ha 'wrug debry; ha a ros radn dha hy gour gensy, hag e 'wrug debry.

7 Ha lagajow anjy veu egerys ha anjy a wodhya dell esa anjy yn noth; ha anjy a wrovas dêlyow fygys warbarth, ha wrovas dhodhans y aprodnyow.

8 Ha anjy a glôwas lev a Arlùth Duw ow kerdhes i'n lowarth in yêynder an dëdh, ha Adam ha'y wreg êth dhe gudha dyworth dyrag an Arlùth Duw in mesk an gwëdh a'n lowarth.

9 Ha'n Arlùth Duw a grias dha Adam ha leverys dhodho: Py le esta?

10 Hag ev a leverys, Me a glôwas dha lev i'n lowarth; ha me a veu own, rag yth esen yn noth, me êth dhe gudha.

§9.2 COLLOQUIAL DOESN'T MEAN CORRUPT

A. Rowe's Genesis 3:11–14 in its original spelling

11 Ha e a gowsas, preg laule theeze tellestah en noath? Aresta debre thort an Gwethan a reeg a vee laule theeeze a na wresta debre?

12 Ha an Deana gowzas, an venin aresta ry dha ve, hy a rose tha ve thor an wethan ha ve reeg debre.

13 Ha an Arleth Deew a gowzas tha an venen, pandrew hemma a eze gwraeze geneze? ha venen a worebaz; An hagar-breeve a thullas ve ha ve reeg debre.

14 Ha an Arleth Deew a lavarras tha an hagar-breeve Drefen chee tha weele hemma tho chee molithes a dres ol an chattel, ha derez kenefra bestaz an gweal; war tha doar chee ra moaze, ha douste chee ra debre oll deethyow tha vownyas.

B. Rowe's Genesis 3:11–14 in KS (*colloquial register*)

11 Ha ev a gowsas, Pyw a wrug lawl dhis 'tell esta yn noth? A wrusta debry dhorth an gwedhen a wruga vy lawl dhis na wresta debry?

12 Ha an den a gowsas, An venyn a wrusta ry dha vy, hy a ros dha vy dhorth an wedhen ha ve 'wrug debry.

13 Ha an Arlùth Duw a gowsas dha'n venyn, Pandra yw hebma eus gwrës genes? Ha'n venyn a worthebas: An hager-brÿv a dùllas vy ha ve 'wrug debry.

14 Ha an Arlùth Duw a lavaras dha'n hager-brÿv: Drefen che dhe wil hebma, yth o'jy molethys a-dres oll an chattel, ha dres kenyver bestas a'n gwel; wàr dha dorr che 'wra mos, ha doust che 'wra debry oll dedhyow dha vôwnans.

C. Rowe's Genesis 3:11–14 in KS (*literary register*)

11 Ha ev a gowsas, Pyw a wrug leverel dhis fatell esta yn noth? A wrusta debry dhyworth an wedhen a wruga vy leverel dhis na wresta debry?

12 Ha'n den a gowsas, An venyn a wrusta ry dhybmo vy, hy a ros dhybmo vy dhyworth an wedhen ha me 'wrug debry.

13 Ha'n Arlùth Duw a gowsas dha'n venyn, Pandra yw hebma eus gwrës genes? Ha'n venyn a worthebys: An hager-brÿv a dùllas vy ha me 'wrug debry.

14 Ha'n Arlùth Duw a leverys dhe'n hager-brÿv: Drefen te dhe wil hebma, yth os jy molethys dres oll an chattel, ha dres kenyver bestas a'n gwel; wàr dha dorr te 'wra mos, ha doust te 'wra debry oll dedhyow dha vôwnans.

9.3 ROWE'S CORNISH TRANSLATION OF MATTHEW 2:1-12

A. Rowe's Matthew 2:1–5 in its original spelling

1 Leben po ve Jesus gennez en Bethalem a Judeah en deethiow Herod an Matern, a reeg doaze teeze veer thor an Est tha Jerusalem.

2 Lavarel, Peleah ma e, yw gennez matern an Ethewan? Rag ma gwellez gen a ni e steran en est, ha tho ni devethez tha gortha thotha.

3 Pereeg Herod an matern clowaz hemma, e ve troublez, ha oll Jerusalem gonz eve.

4 Ha pareg e contell oll an cogazers ewhall ha'n screffars an bobel warbarth e a vednaz thoranze pelle ve Chreest gennez.

5 Ha an gye lavarraz thotha, En Bethalem a Judeah, rag an dellma thewah screffez gen an prophet.

B. Rowe's Matthew 2:1–5 in KS (*colloquial register*)

1 Lebyn pa veu Jesus genys in Bethalem a Jûdêa in dydhyow Herod an mytern, e wrug dos tus fur dhor an Ëst dha Jerùsalem.

2 'Lavaral, Pyle ma e, yw genys mytern an Êdhewon? Rag ma gwelys gena'ny y steren i'n Ÿst, ha th'on ny devedhys dha gordha dhodha.

3 Pa wrug Herod an mytern clôwes hema, e veu troblys, ha oll Jerùsalem gans'ev.

4 Ha pa wrug e cùntell oll an cogasers uhel ha'n screfors a'n bobel warbarth e a 'vydnas dhorans ple veu Crist genys.

5 Ha anjy 'lavaras dhodha, In Bethalem a Jûdêa, rag indelma th'ywa screfys gen an profet:

C. Rowe's Matthew 2:1–5 in KS (*literary register*)

1 Lebmyn pàn veu Jesus genys in Bethalem a Jûdêa in dydhyow Herod an mytern, y whrug dos tus fur dhyworth an Ÿst dhe Jerùsalem.

2 'Leverel, Pyle ma ev, yw genys mytern an Êdhewon? Rag yma gwelys genen ny y steren i'n Ÿst, ha yth on ny devedhys dha wordhya dhodho.

3 Pàn wrug Herod an mytern clôwes helma, ev a veu troblys, ha oll Jerùsalem ganso ev.

4 Ha pàn wrug ev cùntell oll an cogasers uhel ha'n screfors a'n bobel warbarth ev a wovydnas dhyworthans ple feu Crist genys.

5 Ha y a leverys dhodho, In Bethalem a Jûdêa, rag indelma yth ywa screfys gans an profet:

§9.3   COLLOQUIAL DOESN'T MEAN CORRUPT

A. Rowe's Matthew 2:6–10 in its original spelling

6 Ha che Bethalem en Pow Judah neg ooz an behathna amisk maternyow Judah, rag amez a che e ra doaz matern rag rowlya tha pobel Ezarel.

7 Nena Herod, pereg e prevath crya an deeze feere, eve vednaz thoranze seer pana termin reeg an steare disquethaz.

8 Ha e ez devannaz tha Vethalem, ha reeg laule thothonz gworeuh whellas seere râg an flo younk ha parewe why e gavaz, dre geere tha ve arta, mala ve moaze ha gortha thotha aweeth.

9 Perege an gye clowaz an Matern y eath caar, ha an stearan a reeg angye gwellhas en east geeth deractanze ne reeg hi doaze ha savaz derez le ba era an Flo younk.

10 Pereg angye gwellaz an stearan, thonge loan gen meare a loander.

B. Rowe's Matthew 2:6–10 in KS (*colloquial register*)

6 Ha che Bethalem in Pow Jûda, nag os an byhadnha in mysk myternyow Jûda, rag amês a che e wra dos mytern rag rôwlya dha pobel Isarel.

7 Nena Herod, pa wrug e pryveth cria an dus fur, ev 'vydnas dhorans sur pana termyn 'wrug an ster dysqwedhes.

8 Ha e a's davanaz dha Vethalem, ha 'wrug lawl dhodhans: grewgh whelas sur râg an flogh yonk ha pa rewgh why y gavas, drowgh ger dha ve arta, m'ala' ve mos ha gordhya dhodha inwedh.

9 Pa wrug anjy clôwes an mytern y êth 'car, ha an steran a wrug anjy gweles i'n ÿst gêth deractans erna wrug hy dos ha savas dres an leb'era an flogh yonk.

10 Pa' wrug anjy gweles an steren, th'o'njy lowan gen meur a lowender.

C. Rowe's Matthew 2:6–10 in KS (*literary register*)

6 Ha te Bethalem in Pow Jûda, nag os an byhadnha in mysk myternyow Jûda, rag in mes ahanas jy y whra dos mytern rag rôwlya dha bobel Israel.

7 I'n eur-na Herod, pàn wrug ev pryveth cria an dus fur, ev a wovydnas dhyworthans sur pana dermyn 'wrug an ster dysqwedhes.

8 Ha ev a's danvonas dha Vethalem, ha 'wrug leverel dhodhans: gwrewgh whelas sur râg an flogh yonk ha pàn wrewgh why y gavos, drewgh ger dhe vy arta, m'alla' ve mos ha gordhya dhodho inwedh.

9 Pàn wrug anjy clôwas an mytern. y êth in kerdh, ha'n steren a wrussons y gweles i'n Ÿst êth dhyragthans erna wrug hy dos hag a savas dres an le mayth esa an flogh yonk.

10 Pàn wrussons y gweles an steren, yth êns y lowen gans meur a lowender.

A. Rowe's Matthew 2:11-12 in its original spelling

11 ha po tho angye devethez en choy y a wellaz an floh younk gen Mareea e thama, ha angye a gothaz en doer ha gorthaz tha eve. Ha pereg an gye gere go throzor y a rooz thotha aur ha frokensense ha [m]ere.

12 Ha angye ve gwarnez gen Deew ha gye a cuskah ne resa angye doaz ogaz tha Herod, ha anjy eath carr tha pow go honen, vor aral.

B. Rowe's Matthew 2:11-12 in KS (*colloquial register*)

11 Ha pà th'o anjy devedhys i'n chy, y a welas an flogh yonk gen Maria y dhama, ha anjy a godhas i'n dor ha gordhyas dha ev. Ha pa' wrug anjy 'gery gà thresour, y a ros dhodha owr ha frakynsens ha [m]yrr.

12 Ha anjy 'veu gwarnys gen Duw ha anjy o cùsca na resa anjy dos ogas dha Herod, ha anjy êth car dha pow gà honen vordh aral.

C. Rowe's Matthew 2:11-12 in KS (*literary register*)

11 Ha pàn êns y devedhys i'n chy, y a welas an flogh yonk gans Maria y dhama, hag y a godhas dhe'n dor ha gordhyas dhodho ev. Ha pàn wrussons y egery gà thresour, y a ros dhodho owr ha frankynsens ha myrr.

12 Hag y 'veu gwarnys gans Duw hag y ow cùsca na resans y dos ogas dhe Herod, hag y êth in kerdh dh'aga fow gà honen fordh aral.

Generally these extracts, as with all of Wella Rowe's writings, deviate very little from the basic syntax of much contemporary Cornish. The differences are mostly the developments from Middle Cornish—which are to be noted in the bulk of the writing of this era—and in the spelling. Wella Rowe, being a farmer was certainly not a scholar and certainly had not seen a book or document in Cornish before writing these texts. In consequence he wrote and spelt the way in which he spoke Cornish and heard it spoken. This is seen from the way that many verbal particles are either omitted or so spelt that they can be confused one with one another. For example, Rowe rarely writes the verbal particle *a*, for the most part omitting it entirely. And doubtless it was omitted in the speech of all speakers of Cornish. Rowe also knew and used verbal forms introduced by particle *y*, but these are not clearly distinguished in his orthography because he has uses the same spelling for the particle as he uses for other particles or similrly sounding items. In Matthew 2:1 Rowe writes *a reeg doaze*, which from the context is obviously, *y whrug dos* 'there came'. Moreover in

§9.3 COLLOQUIAL DOESN'T MEAN CORRUPT

Matthew 2:6 Rowe writes, *rag amez a che e ra doaz Matern,* which again can be normalized: *rag in mes a jy y whra dos Mytern* 'for out of thee (there) shall come a King'.

Differences other than spelling in Rowe's original text for the most part reflect the way in which the language was developing and in the present author's view, should not, and indeed, cannot be changed for any reason. It is illegitimate to dismiss a development that occurred naturally in the language simply because it does not suit some idealized norm. That was Nance's practice with his Unified Cornish and it haunts us to this day. The changes which can be seen in Rowe's Cornish occurred spontaneously and in accordance with tendencies inherent in the language. They were not decided by some language board's determination of what the members of the board considered acceptable for use by Cornish speakers.

10
SUMMARY

The views which have been set out above may seem to contradict much that is taught and accepted by today's revivalists, but they do represent what is probably the closest approximation to the language of native speakers of Cornish. If this is indeed the case, and the author believes that it is, it is imperative that forms proposed solely to support a particular purist ideal should be ignored—at the very least as far as the spoken language is concerned. Of course it is necessary to examine the Middle Cornish texts closely in order to establish inflected forms, etc., for the revival. Yet it must not be forgotten forget that we are living in the twenty-first century rather than the fourteenth or fifteenth. The spoken Cornish used today must reflect that. Spoken Cornish should be lively, fluent and idiomatic. It should not resemble the language of a sermon in church or chapel!

The object of this book is to show that for a revived language to be as authentic as possible and be accepted as such, it has to follow its natural historical development as a vernacular. There is no possible justification for modern revivalists to tamper with the traditional language as attested. Such meddling with the natural forms of Cornish to force the language to conform to a purist ideal is misguided. Indeed one unfortunate result is that professional linguists dismiss revived Cornish as a spurious construct. The language as we have received it must be accepted as it is. We must revive the language as it was, not as we wish it to have been. There remains, of course, the problem of deciding which exact phase of the language should form the basis for the revived language. The author's preference would be for Cornish as it was in Wella Rowe's day, i.e. towards the end of the seventeenth century. This appears also to have been Jenner's opinion and Jenner is considered by many to have been the best linguist involved in the early stages of the revival.

Of course neologisms are necessary for the modern language, and these should be dealt with as recommended above. We should never lose sight, however, that the essential structure of the sound system and syntax of the

§10

language can be followed. New words, whether borrowed from Welsh and Breton, or English or constructed from native roots do not change the essence of Cornish.

ABBREVIATIONS

AB	Lhuyd, Edward (1707): *Archæologia Britannica*. Oxford. https://ia902701.us.archive.org/35/items/archaeologiabri00lhuygoog/archaeologiabri00lhuygoog.pdf
ACB	Pryce, William (1790): *Archaeologia Cornu-Britannica*. Sherborne. W. Cruttwell. https://ia802909.us.archive.org/14/items/archaeologiacor00prycgoog/archaeologiacor00prycgoog.pdf
BF	Padel, O. J. (1975): *The Cornish Writings of the Bosun Family*. Redruth. Institute of Cornish Studies.
BK	Thomas, Graham & Williams, Nicholas (editors) (2007): *Bewnans Ke: The Life of St Kea*. Exeter. University of Exeter Press.
BM	Stokes, Whitley (editor) (1872): *Beunans Meriasek: The Life of Saint Meriasek*. London. Trübner and Co. https://wikisource.org/wiki/Beunans_Meriasek
Bodinar	William Bodinar's letter. https://en.wikipedia.org/wiki/Cornish_literature
Borde	Borde, Andrew, *The fyrst boke of the introduction of knowledge* (1562) pp 123-25. https://ia801309.us.archive.org/30/items/b21529589/b21529589.pdf
Brome	Brome, Richard (1629): *The Northern Lass:* Act v, Scene ix. https://www.dhi.ac.uk/brome/viewTranscripts.jsp?type=BOTH&play=NL&act=5
Carew	Halliday, F.E. (editor) (1953): *Richard Carew of Antony: The Survey of Cornwall* (1602). London. Andrew Melrose
CW	Stokes, Whitley (editor) (1864): *Gwreans an Bys: The Creation of the World*. https://ia802703.us.archive.org/22/items/gwreansanbyscre01jordgoog/gwreansanbyscre01jordgoog.pdf
Keigwin	John Keigwin, King Charles First's Letter. http://www.moderncornish.net/late-texts/Keigwin-John-kingcharlesfirstletter.html
KS	Kernowek Standard, Standard Cornish
LAM	Kent Alan M. & Saunders, T. (2000): *Looking at the Mermaid*. London. Francis Boutle

OC	Old Cornish
OCV	*Vocabularium Cornicum.* https://wikisource.org/wiki/Vocabularium_Cornicum
OM	*Origo Mundi.* https://wikisource.org/wiki/Origo_Mundi
PA	Pascon agan Arluth. https://wikisource.org/wiki/Pascon_Agan_Arluth
PC	*Passio Christi.* https://wikisource.org/wiki/Passio_Christi
RD	*Resurrexio Domini.* https://wikisource.org/wiki/Passio_Christi
Rowe	Rowe, William, *biblical translations in* Joseph Loth (*editor*), 'Études Corniques', *Revue Celtique* vol. 23 (1902), pp 173-200. https://archive.org/details/revueceltiqu23pari/page/174
SA	*Sacrament an Alter. Thirteenth homily in* Tregear manuscript (TH)
SWF	The Standard Written Form
Symonds	Long, C.E.(editor) (1859): *Richard Symonds's, Diary of the Marches of the Royal Army* (1644), Camden Society. https://archive.org/details/diarymarchesroy00librgoog/page/n101
TH	Homelyes XIII in Cornysche [Homilies of John Tregear]. https://wikisource.org/wiki/Homelyes_XIII_in_Cornysche
WScawen	Williams Scawen (1777): *Observations on an Ancient Manuscript, entitled Passio Christi* [reprinted Gale ECCO print editions (2010)].

SOURCES

[Anon] *Vocabularium Cornicum*. British Library MS Cotton Vespasian Axiv 001-105.
[Anon] *Manuscript Peniarth 105B*. The National Library of Wales.
Borlase, William (1769 [reprinted 1973]): *The Antiquities of Cornwall*. London. E & W Books.
Gover, J. E. B. (1948): *The Place-names of Cornwall*. Truro. Royal Institution of Cornwall.
Jenner, Henry (1904): *A Handbook of the Cornish Language*. London. David Nutt.
Nance, R. M. [various dates] *Collected manuscript notes in the Royal Institution of Cornwall*. Truro.
Nance, R. M. (1938 [reprinted 1970]): *Cornish-English Dictionary*. Redruth. Dyllansow Truran.
Nance, R. M. (1949): *Cornish for All. Revised edition*. St Ives. James Lanham.
Nance, R. M (1952 & 1955 [reprinted 1978]. *Cornish-English & English Dictionary*. The Cornish Language Board, 1978.
Norris, E. (1859), *Ancient Cornish Drama* vol. ii. Oxford. [reprinted 1968. New York/London. Benjamin Blom]
Pryce, W. (1790): *Archæologia Cornu-Britannica*. Sherborne. W. Cruttwell.
Smith, A. S. D. (Caradar) (1947): *The Story of the Cornish Language*. Camborne. Camborne Printing and Stationery Co. Ltd.
Smith, A. S. D. (Caradar) (1972): *Cornish Simplified*. Camborne. An Lef Kernewek.
Tregear, John, (ed.) Bice, C. (1969): *Homelyes in Cornysche*. [*no place*]. published by the editor.
Williams, Nicholas (2014): *Geryow Gwir: The lexicon of Revived Cornish*. Cathair na Mart. Evertype.
Williams, Nicholas (2016): *Studies in Traditional Cornish*. Portlaoise. Evertype.

SYMBOLS

[ ]   Square brackets around a symbol or set of symbols indicate that the sounds in question are to be understood as sounds only, without reference to their function in the sound system of the language.

/ /   Slanted brackets enclose phonemes, that is to say, sounds understood as significant units in the sound system of the language in question. In Late Cornish, for example, [a] and [i] are both members of the same phoneme /ə/.

⟨ ⟩   Angle brackets are used when referring to the way in which a word or sound is written rather than to the way in which it is pronounced.

ː   The triangular colon denotes a long vowel.

ˈ   The vertical line modifier indicates that the following syllable bears the stress, for example, in English *kitten* [ˈkɪtən] or *guitar* [gɪˈtɑːr].

>   X > Y means that X develops into Y.

<   Y < X means that Y develops from X.

*   The asterisk is used to indicate that a form is not actually attested.

a   The vowel of *hat, fat* in the English of Northern English.

æ   The vowel of *hat, fat* in Standard English.

ɑ   The short equivalent of the stressed vowel in Standard English *father*.

dʒ   The sound of *g* in English *badger, magic* or the *j* in *sojourn*.

ð   The sound of *th* in English *this, that, breathe*.

e   "Closed *e*": similar to the first element of the diphthong in *same* [seɪm] or the *é* in French *été*.

ɛ   "Open *e*": approximately the vowel in Standard English *get, pen*.

eɪ   The diphthong heard in Standard English *hate* [heɪt] or *gate* [geɪt].

ə   "Schwa": the neutral vowel of unstressed syllables in English, e.g. in *bigot, onion, brother*, etc.

ᵹ   Insular g, used by Lluyd to indicate the "hard" [g] sound as in *gate*.

i   "Closed *i*": approximately the short equivalent of the vowel in English *screen, feed*.

ɪ   "Open *i*": the vowel in Standard English *bit, sit, bin*. Open *i* [ɪ] and closed *e* [e] are very close to each other.

SYMBOLS

i A centralized i-vowel heard in North Welsh *bydd* 'be', *cudd* 'hidden', etc.

n The sound of English *n* in *no, man, gun*, etc. In Cornish phonology this can be described as a lenis n.

ṇ This was similar to *n* but was pronounced either with more force or with longer duration. It is described as fortis *n*, although its exact phonetic realization is not known.

ɔ "Open *o*": approximately the vowel of Standard English *hot, not*.

ø The vowel in French *cœur* or German *schön*. The short equivalent is written œ.

r̥ The voiceless equivalent of *r*. It can be produced by saying *r* and *h* simultaneously.

u̯ Used by Lhuyd to indicate the consonant [w].

ʌ The sound of *u* in Standard English *up, butter*.

x The sound of *ch* in Scottish *loch* or in the German word *Achtung*.

y The vowel of German *fühlen* or French *vu*. The short equivalent is written ʏ.

ẏ Used by Lhuyd to indicate [ə] or [ʌ].

ȝ The letter yogh, used in Middle Cornish to represent [ð] or [θ]. Not to be confused with ʒ.

ʒ The sound of *s* in such English words as *leisure, pleasure, Asian*.

θ The sound of *th* in English *thick, thin, breath*.

GLOSSARY

analytical: see **synthetic**.

assibilation: when plosives become sibilants the process is known as assibilation. The final segment in Old Cornish tat [taːd] 'father' was assibilated to [z] in Middle Cornish [taːz].

back: back vowels are those that are pronounced with the tongue retracted towards the back of the mouth cavity. [u], [o] and [ɑ] are back vowels

front: front vowels are those that are pronounced with the tongue towards the front of the mouth cavity. [i] and [e] are front vowels.

fronted: a vowel is said to be fronted when as a result of some linguistic change, its articulation has moved from the central or back position to the front.

inflection: inflection is the word used to refer to the various forms taken by a word to show tense, person, gender, number, etc. Inflections are the details of accidence.

lenition: a feature common to all the Celtic languages by which consonants that were originally in intervocalic position were weakend in articulation. Thus in Cornish *an margh* 'the horse' < *sindos markos shows initial m unaffected by any sound change. *An vyrgh* 'the daughter' < *sinda merka shows *v* as the lenition product of *m* between vowels. When a consonant undergoes lenition, it is said to lenite. A learner of Cornish is taught to lenite the initial consonant of a feminine noun after the definite article. Thus he or she will say *benyn* 'woman' but *an venyn* 'the woman', where *venyn* is the lenited form of *benyn*.

lexeme: a word considered as an part of the lexicon of a language.

lexicon: refers to the collection of words in a language. Lexicon is thus the term for the words of a language considered as entries in a dictionary.

mid-high, mid: a vowel is mid-high or a mid vowel when it is between the high vowels and the low vowels. *a* is a low vowel and *i* and *u* are high vowels. *e* and *o* are mid vowels.

mutation: initial mutation refers to the changing of a consonant by lenition or other change. In Cornish *c* becomes *g* by lenition, and *h* by spirantization. Lenition and spirantization are initial mutations.

neologism: a neologism is a word or term newly created to refer to a new idea. Since Cornish ceased to be a community language by the end of the eighteenth century, revivalists have been obliged to coin new words, e.g.

GLOSSARY

pellgowsor 'telephone', *airen* 'aeroplane', *sprusek* 'nuclear' in order to speak about modern notions.

palatalized: consonants are said to be palatalized when they are pronounced with the blade of the tongue against the hard palate. In English the *k* in *kitten* and *kitchen* is a palatalized variant or allophone of the consonant heard in *cool*.

particle: in the Celtic languages a particle is a short and unstressed word that precedes a verb. In Cornish *a*, *y*, *ny*, *na*, and *ow* are particles.

phonology: phonology is that part of linguistic description that concerns itself with the sound system of a language.

possessive adjective: possessive adjectives are those words that precede a noun or noun group and describe who possesses the noun in question. In English *my*, *your*, *his*, *her*, *its*, *our*, and *their* are possessive adjectives.

pre-occlusion: pre-occlusion is that phenomenon in some forms of Cornish by which after a short stressed vowel *n* is preceded by an unexploded *d*, e.g. *penn* 'head' > *pedn* and *m* is preceded by an unexploded *b*, e.g. *mamm* 'mother' > *mabm*.

prepositional pronoun: in the Celtic languages prepositional pronouns are those forms of the personal pronouns that are amalgamated with and form part of the preposition. For example, in Cornish *genef* 'with me', *genes* 'with you', *ganso* 'with him', etc. are all prepositional pronouns.

raising: raising refers to the change of a vowel from one pronounced with the tongue low in the mouth to one that is higher in the cavity. Thus in Cornish the vowel a in *glas* 'blue', for example, is raised from the vowel in, say, Standard English *father* to the vowel in Standard English *glaze*.

rhotacization: this word is based on the word *rho*, the name of the letter *r* in the Greek alphabet. Rhotacization as a phenomenon in phonology refers to the shift of -*s*- [z] between vowels to -*r*-. The most obvious examples in Cornish involve the change of long forms of the verb *bos* 'to be' from *esoma* 'am', *esa* 'was' for example, to *eroma* and *era* respectively.

sibilant: a sibilant is a consonant which seems as it were to hiss. In English *s* and *z* represent sibilants in *sea* and *zoo* for example.

stop: stop is another name for plosive. A plosive or plosive consonant is one in which the airflow is briefly stopped. Thus *p* and *t* are stops, whereas *f* and *th* are continuants.

stressed: a vowel or syllable is stressed when it carries more emphasis than adjacent vowel or syllables. In English for example in the word *relation* [rɪˈleɪʃən] the middle syllable *leɪ* is stressed, *rɪ* precedes the accent and is unstressed, while *ʃən* follows it and is also unstressed.

syntax: syntax is that part of linguistic description that deals with the construction of sentences.

COLLOQUIAL DOESN'T MEAN CORRUPT

synthetic: in the prepositional pronouns forms like *dhym* 'to me' or *dhis* 'to you' are synthetic in that the preposition and the pronoun form a single unit. On the other hand forms like *dhe vy* 'to me' or *dhe jy* 'to you' are analytical being made up of two separate elements, the preposition followed by the relevant pronoun.

unaccented: unaccented means not bearing the stress, unstressed. See **stressed**.

unexploded: when pre-occlusion first occurred the *d* before the *n* and the *b* before the *m* were unexploded. That is to say the speaker produced the beginning of the *d* or *b* but did not complete it before producing the *n* or *m*. Later the d or b was fully exploded and indeed swamped the following n or m. Thus hedna became hedda, and lebmyn became lebbyn.

unrounding: a vowel is rounded if it is formed by pursing the lips. If the lips are spread rather than pursed the vowel is not rounded. In Cornish the original vowel in *tus* 'men' or *cul* 'narrow' was similar to the vowel of the French words *lune* 'moon' or *vu* 'seen'. Later the Cornish vowel unrounded to a sound similar to the vowel in English *sheet* or *seen*. *Tus* was the original form, but the later forms *tees* and *teez* show an unrounded vowel.

unstressed: unstressed is another word for unaccented.

velar fricative: the sound of *gh* in Cornish *flogh* 'child' is a voiceless velar fricative [x]. Velar means that it is pronounced as the back of the oral cavity or velum. It is a fricative because it makes a sort of rubbing sound.

vernacular: the vernacular means the commonly spoken language; vernacular is also an adjective, so one can say, for example, that Cornish revivalists are attempting to recapture the sounds and syntax of traditional Cornish when it was a vernacular language.

vicesimal: many of the Celtic languages have a tendency to count in twenties. Thus in Cornish, for example, 'sixty' is *try ugans* i.e. three twenties and 'eighty' is *peswar ugans* 'four twenties'. This method of counting is called the vicesimal system from Latin vicesimus 'twentieth'.

voiced: a voiced consonant is one that is pronounced both in the oral cavity and with vibration of the vocal chords. Thus *b* and *d* are both voiced, whereas there voiceless equivalents *p* and *t* are pronounced without any such vibration.

voiceless: a consonant is voiceless when the vocal chords do not vibrate while it is being articulated.

INDEX

a 'from' 6.3, 6.5.6
abarth 'on behalf of' 3.18
abrans 'eyebrow' 4.2
agan 'our', *agas* 'your', *aga* 'their' > *gàn, gàs, gà* 3.2
agas eskyjyow why 'your shoes' > *gas skyjyow why* 3.2
angy, anjy 'they'; pronoun ignored by Nance 6.1; examples of *anjy* from the later texts 6.2
analogical forms disregarded 2.8
Anglo-Saxon 7.5; Anglo-Saxon period 1.1
Antiquities of Williams Borlase 2.4
archaism in indirect statement 2.8; archaizing inflection 2.8; archaism in inflection with modern neologisms 7.4
Archæologia Cornu-Britannica 4.1
arhans 'silver' 3.15; mistakenly 'money'; mispronounced **arkans* 3.8; *arghans* in the texts 3.15.1; *arhans* 3.15.2; *arans* 3.15.3; 'silver' only 7.1-7.1.1
assibilation 3.5
autonomous forms of the verb 5.1; in *Pascon agan Arluth* 5.1.1; in *Origo Mundi* 5.1.2; in *Passio Christi* 5.1.3; in *Resurrexio Domini* 5.1.4; in *Bewnans Ke* 5.1.5; in *Bewnans Meriasek* 5.1.6
a wrusta mos? 'did you go?' 3.2
bê for **begh* 'load' in the texts 3.17
bean 'small' 3.9.4
bedneth 'blessing' but *banneth* without pre-occlusion 3.25
beghan 'small' 3.9.1, 6.1.3

Berryman, Mrs 2.1
Bewnans Meriasek 2.6; pre-occlusion in 3.26
Bewnans Ke 2.6
bian 'small' 3.9.5
Bodinar, William 2.3
bogh 'cheek' 4.1
bohosogyon ~ bohojogyon 'poor people' 3.5
Borde, Andrew 3.27
Borlase, William 2.4, 5.9
bos 'to be'; *boys* 3.4.3; personalized forms of the verbal noun 5.3; 1st pers. sg. *bosa, bosaf, bosama* 5.3.1; 2nd pers. sg. *bota, bosta* 5.3.2; 3rd pers. sg. masc. *bosa* 5.3.3; 3rd pers. sg. fem. *bossy* 5.3.4; 1st pers. pl. *bosen* 5.3.5; 2nd pers. pl. *bosowgh* 5.3.6; 3rd pers. pl. *bosans* 5.37
Boson, John 3.4
Boson, Nicholas 2.3, 3.4
Bosporthennis (Zennor), Pordhunes vyan 3.10
Bosullow (Wendron), Bossewolouvyan 3.10
Boswednack 2.1, 2.2
Botheras, William 2.1
brâs 'great'; written ⟨broaz⟩ and ⟨brose⟩ 3.4; *brosyen* 'important people' 3.4
brehow 'arms' 4.7.2
Breton; no assibilation in 3.5
Brome, Richard 3.27
bu for *be* 2.5
byan, byen 'small' 3.9.3
*byghan 'small' 3.8; 3.9 mispronounced **bykan* 3.8, 3.10, 6.1.3

111

byhan 'small' 3.9.2
Cambridge 2.5
cân 'song', written ⟨caon⟩ 3.4
Caradar see Smith, A. S. D.
Cardiff 2.2
Cardinham (Crowan), Cardynan Vyan 3.19
Carew, Richard 3.27
Cargeeg, Francis 2.5
Carvear (St Blazey) 3.2
Carwythenak 3.17
Celtic Congress 2.2
Chyvarloe (Gunwalloe) 3.17.3
Cornish-English Dictionary by Nance (1938) 2.7
Cornish for All 2.5
counting in Cornish 8
Creation of the World (*Gwreans an Bys*) 2.5, 2.6; pre-occlusion in 3.27
Creeglaze 3.4
crysy/*crygy* 'to believe' 3.6
'cute' in English 3.3
Davey, John 2.2
deg milblek 'ten thousand times' 8
del, *dell* 'as' introducing indirect speech 5.2
deus 'come' written ⟨dus⟩, ⟨des⟩, ⟨dees⟩ 3.3
dewdhorn 'hands' 4.2.1, 4.9.2; *dornow* 'fists, hands' 4.9.2
dewdros 'feet' and *treys* 4.3.1
dewfrik 'nose' 4.1; 4.11.1
dewlagas 'eyes' 4.1; 4.4.1
dewlyn 'knees' 4.10.1
*dewotty, *dywotty 'public house,' a spurious coinage 7.2
dhe, *the* 'to' 6.3, 6.4, 6.5.1
dhedhans, *dhodhans* 'to them' 6.3, 6.4.5
dhyrag, *dyrag* 'before, in front of' 6.5.9
dhyworth, *dhort* 'from' 6.3, 6.5.4
difference; phonetic difference between *r* < *rdh* and *r* < *rth* 3.19
dorn 'fist, hand' 4.2
dos 'to come; *doys* 3.4.3
dre 'through' 6.5.11

duals; unattested but recommended by Nance and others 2.8, 4.1
Dunmeer (Bodmin) 3.3
Duporth (St Austell) 3.3
duth for *deth* 2.5
*dywarr 'two legs' unattested in Cornish 4.5.1
dywla, *dewla* 'hands' 4.2.2
*dywscovarn 'two ears' unattested in Cornish 4.6.1
*dywvordhos 'two thighs' unattested in Cornish 4.11
dywscoth 'shoulders' 4.8.1
dywvregh 'arms' 4.7.1
eâ 'yes' 5.7
East Looe (St Martin-by-Looe) 3.17.3
ehen 'sort, kind'; spelt *eghen* by Nance and SWF 3.13; *eghen* in the texts 3.13.1; *ehen* in the texts 3.13.2
English language 1.1; words: *gate*, *hate* 3.4.2
er 'by' 5.10
eran, *eranny* for *eson*, *eson ny* 3.25
ergh 'snow' as *yrth* 3.21
esa 'was' > *era* 3.25; *esoma* 'I am', *eson* 'we are' > *eram*, *eran* 3.25
ev a welas 'he saw' 3.2
Falmouth 2.4
fas 'face' 3.4
fatel, *fatell* 'how' introducing indirect speech 5.2
'feet' in Cornish 4.3; 'hands and feet' in Cornish 4.3
'fists, hands' in Cornish 4.9
flehes 'children'; mispronounced *flekes 3.8; spelt *fleghes* by Nance 3.12; *fleghas*, *fleghes* in the texts 3.12.1; *flehas*, *flehes* in the texts 3.12.2
forth, *fordh* 'road, way' 3.18
French 7.5; *cœur* 'heart', *sœur* 'sister' 3.3; *blé* 'corn', *pré* 'meadow 3.3
frigow 'nose' & *dewfrik* 4.1; 4.11.2
gallosek ~ *gallogek* 'powerful' 3.5
gans, *gen* 'with' 6.3, 6.5.2; *gansans* 'with them' 6.3, 6.5.2

INDEX

garr 'leg' 4.1; *garrow* 'legs' 4.5.2
gasa 'to let' > *gara* 3.25
gerys 'let' for *gesys* 3.25
gest 'bitch' 3.4
⟨gh⟩ in revived Cornish spelling 3.8; the sound [x] lost finally 3.17; final *gh* written as ⟨th⟩ 3.21
glas 'blue' 3.4; *glays* 3.4.3
Glasney (Budock) 3.22
glinyow 'knees' 4.10.2
godhvos 'to know'; negative imperfect *ny wodhyen, na o'yen* 5.5; **godhyr* 'is known' unattested; *yth yw* but *bos* + *gothvethys* 'is known' is attested 5.1.6
Goonamarth (St Mewan) 3.21
gortheby, gorreby 'to answer' 3.20.1
gorthuwher 'evening'; mispronounced **gorthuger* 3.14; **gorthugher* unattested 3.14.1; *gorthuwher*, etc. 3.14.2
gorthyp, gorryb 'answer' 3.20.2
Gothers (St Dennis), Gudefosbian 3.10
Great Vowel Shift 3.4.1
Greek 2.5, 5.9
Gwavas, William 2.3
gul 'to do' written ⟨gîl⟩ and ⟨gweel⟩ 3.3; *gwrug* 'did' 3.3
gwâv 'winter' 3.4
gwelv 'lip' 4.1
gwewen 'heel' 4.1
gwews 'lip' 4.1
Hall, Richard 2.1
Handbook of the Cornish Language 2.1, 2.2, 2.3
'hands' in Cornish 4.2
Henfordh > Henvor 3.18
henna 'that' > *hedna, hedda* 3.26; Lhuyd's *hana* ~ *hedda* 3.26
Higher Boswarva 2.2
'horseman, knight' 3.11.1; 'horsemen, knights' 3.11.2
in 'in' 6.5.3; *in an sy* 'in them' for **in anjy* 6.1
indirect statement; methods for forming 5.2; indirect speech with *del* 5.2.1; indirect speech with *fatel* 5.2.2
initial mutations; absent in *Pascon agan Arluth* 3.23; absent in some toponyms 3.24
in kerth, in kerdh, in ker 'away' 3.18.2
Jenner, Henry 2.1, 2.7, 3.2; and the start of the revival 2.2
Jordan, William 2.5
Kellybray (Stoke Climsland) 3.17.3
kerensa/kerenja 'love' 3.6
kerhes 'to fetch, to bring'; *kerghes* in the texts 3.16.1; *kerhes* 3.16.2; *keres* 3.16.3
kerthes, kerdhes, kerras 'to walk' 3.18
kews for *cows* 2.5
King Charles's letter 8
lagasow 'eyes' 4.1; 4.4.2; *lagagow anjy* 'their eyes' 6.1
Landrine (Ladock), Landreynbyan 3.10
language change 3
Lannarth 3.21
Late Cornish 2.2, 2.3, 2.4
Latin 2.5, 5.9
'legs' in Cornish 4.5
lemmyn 'now' > *lebmyn, lebbyn* 3.26
lenis *n* /n/ ~ fortis *n* /ṇ/ 3.26
leun, luen 'full' > ⟨lene⟩ 3.3
leuw 'hand' 4.2; dual *dywla* 4.2, 4.3
lexicon: problems in 7
Lhuyd, Edward 3.3, 5.9
Loe Bar (Sithney) 3.17.3
long *a* in Cornish 3.4
Looe (the River) 3.17.3
Lord's Prayer 2.1
loss of *th* after *r* 3.18; loss of final ⟨th⟩ after a vowel 3.22
Luxulyan < *Lok Sulyan* 3.3; 3.22
Madron 2.2
mamm 'mother' > *mabm* 3.26; *mamb* in *Sacrament an Alter* 3.26
Mann, John 2.1
margh 'horse' as *marth* 3.21

COLLOQUIAL DOESN'T MEAN CORRUPT

marhak, marhek 'knight, horseman', pl. *marghogyon* 3.11.1-2; spelt *mar(gh)ak* by Nance 2.8, 3.8
marhogeth 'to ride' in the texts 3.11.3
marthojyon, marojyon 'wonders' 3.20.3
ma sagh vy wàr an bùss 'my bag's on the bus' 3.2
me a wra 'I shall' 3.2
me yw gylwys 'I am called' 5.1
Menacuddle 3.22
Menadue (Tintagel) 3.22; Menadue (St Breward) 3.22
Menedu (Luxulian) 3.22
Menna (St Dennis) 3.22
metanalysis or false division 6.1
Middle Cornish 2.2, 3.1; Middle and Late Cornish overlap 2.3; surviving Middle Cornish texts 2.6
Middle English 5.9
Mid-Wales 3.4.1
mil 'thousand' 8; *dyw vil* 'two thousand' 8; *teyr mil* 'three thousand' 8; *milyow cans* 'a hundred thousand' 8
milweyth 'a thousand times' 8
Minnimeer (Tremaine) 3.3; 3.22
"Modern Cornish" 2.2
mona 'money' not *arhans* 7.1.2
mordhosow 'thighs' 4.1; 4.12.2
mos 'to go'; *moys* 3.4.3
mylyon: *try mylyon* 'three million' 8
myrgh 'daughter' as *mirth* 3.21
myjy 'to reap' 3.8
nâ 'no' 5.7
nag eus 'is not' Late for *nynj eus* 3.7
Nance, R.M 2.2, 2.6; his approach to Cornish 2.4; his *Cornish-English Dictionary* of 1938 2.6; his unfortunate legacy 2.8; ignores *s/j* variation 3.6
Nancemeor (St Clements) 3.3
Nancledra 2.4
Nanpean (St Stephen in Brannel), Nanspian 3.10; (St Stephen in Brannel, St Just in Penwith, Stithians) 3.24

Nanspean (Gunwalloe, St Enoder) 3.24; Nansbyan 3.10
nans/nanj 'now, already' 3.6
neologisms 7.5
nep pell for *napell* 2.5
Newlyn 2.1
Norman Conquest 7.5
Norris, Edwin 5.4
North-West of Ireland 3.4.1
'nose, nostrils' in Cornish 4.11
numeration; a suggested revision to the Cornish system 7.1
nyns/nyng 'not' 3.6; examples in Middle Cornish 3.7
Old Cornish 2.2
Old English (Anglo-Saxon) 5.9
Ordinalia, the 2.6
Origo Mundi 2.6
orth 'at' 6.5.5
particles: *a, y* & *ow* 3.2
Pascon agan Arluth 2.6; *nynj* universal in 3.6
Passio Christi 2.6
pedren 'buttock' 4.1
Penhallick (Illogan), Penhellekbyan 3.10
Penmennor (Stithians) 3.22
penn 'head' > *pedn* 3.26
place-names; with unrounded *u* 3.3; with unrounded *ue, eu* 3.3
pluperfect after *Pascon agan Arluth* used only as conditional 5.6; first noticed by Norris (1859) 5.6
Pol Glaze 3.4
Polgrain (St Wenn) 3.3, 3.10
Polgreen (St Veep) 3.3
Polpear (Lelant) 3.3
Polzeath 3.21
porth 'harbour' 3.18
Porthbean (St Keverne, Gerrans, St Anthony in Roseland) 3.24
Porthhallow 3.18
Porthpean (St Austell) 3.24
Porthoustock 3.18
Portlooe (Talland) 3.17

INDEX

possessive adjectives: emphatic pronoun used for 3.2
pre-occlusion 3.26; repudiated by Nance 2.8; absent from Tregear 3.26; in *Beunans Meriasek* 3.27.1; in Andrew Borde 3.27.2; in *Sacrament an Alter* 3.27.3; in Richard Carew 3.27.4; in *Creation of the World* 3.27.5; in Richard Brome 3.27.6; in Richard Symonds 3.27.7; in Wella Rowe 3.27.8
prepositions 6.1
prepositional pronouns; simplification of 6.3; with *the* 'to' in the texts 6.4.1-5; recommended forms of 6.5
Priske (Mullion), Preskebyan 3.10
Pryce, William 4.1, 7.2
pysy ~pygy 'to pray' 3.5
questions and answers 7.3
quiescent letters maintained 2.8
Rablen, Arthur 2.1
rag 'for' 6.3, 6.5.8; *ragthans* 'for them' 6.3
ras 'grace'; *rays* 3.4.3
Resurrexio Domini 2.6
rhotacization 3.25
'ride' (verbal noun) 3.11.3
Rowe, Wella; pre-occlusion in 3.26; his Cornish 9.1; his translation of Genesis iii. (2-14) 9.2; his translation of St Matthew's Gospel ii.(1-12) 9.3
rth > r, rr 3.20; phonetic difference between *r < rdh* and *r < rth* 3.19
ryb 'beside' 6.5.10
Sacrament an Alter 2.6, 3.26, 3.27
sagh vy 'my bag' 3.2
St Columb 2.2
St Just 2.1
saw 'load' 3.17.2
Scarrabine (St Endellion) 3.10
scodhow 'shoulders' 4.8.2
scovornow 'ears' 4.1, 4.6.2
Shakespeare 5.9
'Sketch of Cornish Grammar' 4.5

Skewes (St Wenn), Skywysbian 3.10
'small' (*byan*, etc.) in place-names 3.10
Smith, A. S. D. Nance's collaborator and critic 2.5; proponent of medieval Cornish 2.7
sound system of Cornish 3.1
South Welsh 3.4.1
spelling changed without warrant 2.8
Standard Written Form (SWF) 2.7, 3.8, 3.12
Story of the Cornish Language, The 2.7
summary 10
survivals of the traditional Cornish 2.1
Symonds, Richard 3.27
tâl 'forehead' 3.4
tas 'father' 3.4; *tays* 3.4.3
tavern 'public house' 7.2
Tencreek (Menheniot) 3.3; (Lansallos) 3.3; (St Veep) 3.3
⟨th⟩ lost finally after a vowel 3.22
the 'to'; *the gy* 'to you' (sg.) 6.4.2; *the ny* 'to us' 6.4.3; *the vy* 'to me' 6.4.1; *the why* 'to you' (pl.) 6.4.3, 6.4.4; *thothans, thethans* 'to them' 6.4.5
Tolgus (Redruth) 3.3, 3.10
'tongue' meaning 'language' 3.1
Tonkin, Thomas 4.1
Trebiffin (Lesnewth), Trebyan 3.10
Trebyan (Lanhydrock) 3.10
Tregear, John 2.5; Tregear's *Homilies* 2.5, 2.6; shows no examples of pre-occlusion 3.26
Tregoose (Feock) 3.3
Tregoose (St Erth),Tregosbyan 3.10
Tremail 3.24
Tremar 3.24
Tremayne (St Gennys, Crowan & St Columb Major) 3.24
Tremeer 3.24
Tremethick 3.24
Tremewan 3.24
Trenance (Mullion), Trenansbyan 3.10
Trencreek (Creed) 3.3; (Veryan) 3.3
Trengilley (Constantine), Trekellybyan 3.10

Trequite (St Kew), Tregoydbyan 3.10
Tresmeer (Tresmeer) 3.3
Trevean (Morva), Trevian 3.10
Trevean (Newlyn East), Drefvyan 3.10
Trevear (Sennen) 3.3
Trevenna (St Mawgan) 3.22
Trevine (St Minver), Trevyan 3.9
Trevorva (Probus) 3.2
Trewarmenna (Creed) 3.22
Trewarnveneth (Paul) 3.22
Treweeg (Stithians) 3.3, 3.10
Trewirgie (Redruth) 3.3
tron 'nose' not in Middle Cornish 4.1
treys 'feet' 4.3.2; *treys ha dewla* 'feet and hands' 4.3.2-3
tus 'men' 3.3
pronunciation of long *a* 3.4
ufern 'ankle' 4.1
unaccented syllables 3.2
Unified Cornish 2.5, 2.6
unstressed vowels retained 2.8
usy/ugy 'is' 3.6
variation between *s* and j, *g* 3.5; ignored by Nance 3.6
Ventonveth (Veryan) 3.21
verbs 5
vernacular 3.1

vicesimal system of counting 7.1
Vingoe, Mrs Elizabeth 2.2
Vounder (Mullion), Boundervian 3.10
Vownder Goth 3.18
vowels: Middle Cornish *u* unrounded to [i] 3.3; Middle Cornish *eu*, *ue* unrounded to [e] 3.3.
vyden in *me a vyden gewel* 'I will do' (Borde) 3.26
Wales 2.4
wàr 'upon' 6.5.7
warlergh 'after, according to' as *warlerth*, *warlyrth* 3.21.1
Welsh 2.5; no assibilation in 3.4; *traed a dwylo* 'hands and feet' in 4.3
whath, *wheth* 'yet' 3.4
whe 'six' 3.17.1,
y (particle) 3.2; *y* (possessive adjective) 3.2
y'm gylwyr 'I am called' 5.1
yma, *ma* (not *eema) 3.2
y whelyr, y whylyr 'is seen' 5.1
z ⟨s⟩ between vowels does not become *g 3.5
z ⟨s⟩ > *r* (rhotacization) 3.25
Zennor 2.1

www.ingramcontent.com/pod-product-compliance
Lightning Source LLC
LaVergne TN
LVHW011424080426
835512LV00005B/260